EMPOWER
BUSINESS
EVERYWHERE

HOW TO CHANGE THE WORLD WITH YOUR WHY

TRACY REPCHUK

with

Gary Stuart | Bruce Keith | Vivian De Guzman | Shirley Dalton | Donya Fahmy
Paramahansa Jagadish | Suzi Nelsen | Andrena Taylor | Shkira Singh

Other Works with Tracy Repchuk

 *Start Right Marketing*

31 Days to Millionaire Marketing Miracles

 *The Poetry of Business*

Quantum Leap Your Life

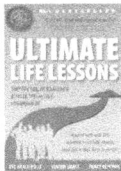 *Ultimate Life Lessons*

25 Brilliant Business Mentors

 *Ready, Aim, Inspire*

Discover more at
http://TracyRepchuk.com

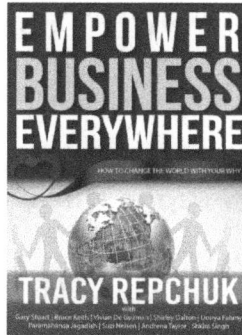

Empower Business Everywhere
How to Change the World with Your Why

Tracy Repchuk

Co-authored with

Gary Stuart • Bruce Keith
Vivian De Guzman • Shirley Dalton
Donya Fahmy • Paramahansa Jagadish
Suzi Nelsen • Andrena Taylor • Shkira Singh

QuantumLeapAuthor.com

Dedication and Acknowledgements

I would like to dedicate this book to those who are living on purpose, mission, and creating their vision so that they can live free, and help others do the same, especially the natural healers, activists, and game changers.

In addition, I'd like to thank those who support them—and of course me—so we can lead, participate, and connect with amazing people, just like you. When we have support from family, friends, associates, mentors, coaches, mastermind groups, and followers, it gives us the luxury of time to do projects like this.

Special acknowledgements to those who have become a sacred part of my journey, learning, and respect:

Mark Anastasi, Richard Branson, Hilary Clinton, Joel Comm, Tom Cruise, Antonio Gellini, Seth Godin, Teresa de Grosbois, Ken McArthur, Armand Morin, Lisa Nichols, Kym Yancey, Sandra Yancey, Oprah Winfrey.

Enjoy the book and connect with each of us!

Tracy Repchuk,
International Bestselling Author and Speaker

Contents

Chapter 1

The Time to Empower is NOW!
by Tracy Repchuk

There are seven billion people in the world, three billion of them are online and five billion are using mobile phones, so if you ever wanted to reach millions with your message—the technology exists right now. So, I ask you this question: are you really using it?

I started my entrepreneurial journey at the age of nineteen, when I graduated with a degree in IT and started a software company. I broke into a world where men dominated.

I don't know about you, but I did not have the vision, purpose, and mission that I do now. I had one goal—to make a million dollars.

By twenty-four I had made my first million and was developing systems for the government, national banks, the lottery corporation, and fortune 100 companies.

In fact, once the Internet was born, and already in 1994 I was developing software and websites for clients, and was one of the first 100,000 sites on the Internet.

But that didn't mean my journey was not without tragedy. By the time I was twenty-four, I had been left at the altar with a broken heart by my fiancé/business partner. I married on

1

the rebound and divorced in under a year; I had to move back home with my parents because my business partner/ex fiancé locked me out of my business and stopped my credit cards, and my soon-to-be ex-husband did the same at home. I am often asked how I survived this.

You see, I knew I had a mission and a purpose to use my skills and knowledge of technology to break barriers for change agents. I took out loans to buy my ex-fiancé out of my business. I took out loans to get my ex-husband out of my life.

I would not be silenced because if I was, then other woman would be too. When you know that your mission is bigger than yourself, getting up is the easy part.

I got myself on TV, I got myself to #1 on Amazon.com, I won new Internet marketing success of the year (the first woman to win that), I was flown—all expenses paid—from California to Singapore to appear on my very first stage, in front of 34,00 people as the prize, and I paved the way as the only woman on the World Internet Summit stages—with fifteen men.

I got picked up by Wiley Publishing and became a five-time international bestselling author. Then I got myself on TV over and over and over and traveled around the world to over thirty-five countries, speaking on this topic.

I even opened up the first business women's center in Kuwait, because that was the first time they had the right to own their own business, and a privilege we take for granted.

I speak about this to tell you need to play a bigger game. You need to speak up, and you need to get your message heard by millions.

Play a Bigger Game

In most cases you are living under the illusion of your comfort zone, which you think is like a beachside hammock, when in reality it's a closed, cramped, box.

And outside of your comfort zone, awaits your dreams.

I know it's outside of your comfort zone because if they were inside your comfort zone, EVERYBODY would be happy.

Have you ever seen the movie the Matrix? This is the reality of your comfort zone. I know this from experience because speaking, networking, and anything where I am out from behind my computer, is outside of my comfort zone. So now I am living comfortably uncomfortable knowing I am always ready for a bigger game.

Here's why you need to use technology to get your message out now.

It's because if you are reading this, you are a change agent. You are possibly a healer, a speaker, an author, or an entrepreneur who is socially responsible, challenges boundaries, and takes risks. You care for the people of this planet and the planet itself. Am I right?

Automatically Attract Your Ideal Client

This is where most businesses fail; they fail to identify specifically who they are marketing to . . . age, demographics, interests—what is called a customer avatar. How can you attract your ideal client when you haven't identified them? Here is why you must know that information in today's market. If you don't, you can't create content for them using the language they will relate to and understand. You can't establish colors for your brand, because you don't know what their expectations are. You can't find where they are,

3

because you serve everyone. Serving everyone is a surefire way to not be found, heard, seen, or chosen online. You must truly identify your market and create the atmosphere and environment they expect, relate to, and understand. Now you can go to Google and find out what they are thinking and saying, so you can grab the keywords to use on your site. Keywords are the key to using SEO (search engine optimized) phrases that will attract Google.

The second element is to separate yourself by defining a Unique Selling Proposition (USP), so prospects understand why they should choose you, and what makes you different.

My USP is, *"Get a Fully Branded Online Web Presence and Message to Market System in Under 60 Days."*

My target market is forty to sixty-year old professional women who are game-changers and want to play bigger and leave their legacy, and who don't want to deal with technology. They want a fully branded done-for-you website created with marketing results in mind, with someone to maintain it, and guide them through all the obstacles they will encounter.

Because I know that— I know where they are, what they are doing, and what their pain points are— I know how to find their keywords and use them in their materials.

Be Prepared

I advise all of my clients to build their website around the person they want to be five years from now, because that physically manifests it today! I had my site ready, I looked like a speaker, and I got booked. I also discovered that money loves speed, and it's better to be ready for your Oprah moment well before it comes—because when it comes, life moves too quickly. The first issue to address is whether or not you "professionally match," which means you look as good

4

online as you do off. When someone meets you at an event, and you look good, they are eager to do business with you and refer you. They take your business card, and guess what they are going to do . . .

Look at Your Website

You have three seconds to make an impression and *"If your websites aren't working for you—they're working against you!"*

So your site needs effective branding, navigation, layout, design, marketing strategy for every page, effective targeting for an end result for every page, an objective, a profile of you as an authority (speaker, author, etc), and everything else you need in order to rise above the competition.

But then that's only one-half a strategy. The Grand Kahuna of your business should become your landing page.

A landing page is a two page website; one page exchanges a gift for a name and email address, and the second page thanks them, provides them with the gift, and prompts them to take their next action.

This page is vital to list-building. Your business needs to handle the inflow of prospects from online, communicate automatically on your behalf, and then prepare them to easily be "closed" through a call with you, or if the products and services are lower priced, through the information on your website and email education.

You need this page so you can create a community of people who know, like, and trust you. It provides you with the ability to promote from your social media sites, your blog, radio, telesummits, and your live appearances; you can send them to your landing page, and actually track and monitor and be able to build a relationship with the people who are interested in what you have. When you send someone directly to your master website, you have no way of knowing if they found what they were looking for, who they were, if they had any questions, or if they were interested in finding out more information—*nothing*—they are *gone*! And because the average sale takes seven touch points, you are a long way off from closing and converting them.

It was this page that created for me the massive success I have had. I became a #1 bestseller because of this page. I convert and make money while I sleep because of this page, and I have an ability to communicate automatically, educate and enlighten people on my products and services, and make them comfortable about making a purchase.

So before you spend any more money on traffic, websites, or branding, make sure you have a separate landing page that is preparing you for success.

Reach Millions with Your Message

The four primary categories I used to reach on average twenty million people last year alone, was the combination of:

1. Internet and online branding and marketing

2. Book launch for credibility and market differentiation

3. Speaking

4. TV

The only thing left is social media, which I want to cover in a bit more detail.

Social media falls under the Internet marketing element, but I wanted to save it until we addressed the landing page, because if you don't have a landing page, where are you sending your traffic and connections to?

Social media is different than other online marketing activities because the purpose of it is to engage an audience, not necessarily sell to them. That comes later when you create a community of people who know you, like you, trust you, and ultimately buy from you. This is why sending them to your landing page and moving them to the next step of the relationship is so important.   Before social media, we did not have this power to impact millions in minutes. That dream now exists.

There are a lot of social media platforms, but four which I focus on:

1. LinkedIn

2. Facebook

3. Twitter

4. Google

The key is to understand what each is used for to determine where you should be spending your time.

LinkedIn

If you are in a profession at all, you need to be on LinkedIn. Currently I have over 12,000 followers here, and they are incredibly responsive. There are tons of benefits to LinkedIn, but the two that people may not be aware of is there are specific groups you can join that can make you money. For example, I have gotten many speaking engagements from LinkedIn by being part of groups such as *Need a Speaker*. Groups exist for almost every niche, field, product or service.

The second benefit is that there is often research there (by an organization or group) that you can use for your own target marketing. For example, carpet cleaners have a group there that assists people in that industry to understand what is happening and what they need to focus on.

You can connect with me on LinkedIn here:
https://www.linkedin.com/in/tracyrepchuk

Facebook

Facebook is the platform for relationship building. Its structure makes it easy to connect, engage, participate, and follow a conversation. You can create personal pages, groups, a company site, and where I spend most of my time is in my private Facebook group for upper level clients. It's a great way to remain accessible and connected to your followers.

Connect with me on Facebook here:
https://www.facebook.com/TracyRepchukFan

Twitter

The other way I use social media, particularly Twitter, is to drive traffic to my landing pages, so that I fill my own funnel. You must realize that with a social media platform such as Facebook or Twitter, any followers you have aren't really yours, so you need to get them into your own database. If Twitter wanted to close your account today, they could. So if you became dependent just on social media such as Twitter for leads or for your marketing, you are depending on a fragile structure. It's like building your house out of straw. I have never seen a greater or faster way than Twitter to specifically locate and target your audience for free, engage them, and pull them into your own funnel, which is why it can't be ignored as a business practice.

Connect with me on Twitter here:
https://twitter.com/tracyrepchuk

Google+

Google+ is a relative newcomer to the game of social media but with a name like Google, it doesn't take much to change the game. They have combined the power of other platforms, and created an environment that is ideal for businesses. Make sure you add this to your portfolio, and get familiar with their features.

But the big difference and the real reason you need Google+ is . . . drum roll . . . it's the only social media platform that indexes your post to Google, giving you the SEO power you want for free. With its plan for Internet domination, and with $200 billion in its pockets, it will probably succeed and you want to be at the forefront of this wave.

Connect with me on Google + here:
https://plus.google.com/u/0/+TracyRepchukTV

So, I hope you have gotten a broad overview of how to create an online presence where you professionally match, rise above the competition, and reach millions with your message.

I invite you to connect with me and let me help you.

If you would like me to guide or take your technology off your plate—do your online branding, website development, landing page, market funnel, logo, consult with you, be your partner, and mastermind, then connect with me here to get familiar with my offerings.

www.FastActionResults.com

I look forward to starting a relationship with you, finding out more about what you do, and about your vision, purpose, and mission, so I can serve you in the deepest way possible.

Look on the next page for a special FREE gift I have for you.

I'll see you on the inside.

Tracy Repchuk

F@st Action
Result$

Tracy's Special Offer:

Are You Tired of Wasting Time Online,
Spending Good Money After Bad,
and Totally Overwhelmed?

Ready to FAST-TRACK your results? Let me help . . .

For more detail than I could give here, grab my *Free Guide:*

How Your Brand, Websites,
and Social Media Work Together

This info-packed guide takes you through the
Five Steps to Instant Online Impact
to understand how your brand, websites,
and social media all work together.

GET IT NOW AT

www.FastActionResults.com

11

Internet + Social Media Speaker

Meet Tracy Repchuk

Tracy Repchuk is an online marketing and social media strategist and speaker. She's an International best-selling author, and has been an award-winning entrepreneur since 1985. She has helped thousands of clients get their message out around the world. Tracy is an internationally acclaimed speaker and motivator in over thirty-five countries. She keeps audiences engaged with her ability to break down complex concepts and turn them into formula-based success.

Tracy started her first software business at the age of nineteen, which still supports Fortune 100 companies. She has been nominated for awards such as "Entrepreneur of the Year," "Chamber of Commerce Business Woman of the Year," "Coach of the Year," and *Stevie Awards* for "Business Mentor of the Year." She has received "Provincial Volunteer" and software development awards. She is a seven-time international best-selling author, an internationally acclaimed speaker, and a sought-after motivator in over thirty-five countries. In addition, Tracy is an award winning speaker, entrepreneur, writer, software developer, and Internet marketer—including commendations from the White House. She has also appeared in the *International Who's Who* in seven categories.

Tracy graduated in Business Computer Systems, and went on to receive a Certified Management Accountants designation. In 2007, she won "New Internet Marketing Success of the Year" from the World Internet Summit, and catapulted into success with her best-selling book—*31 Days to Millionaire Marketing*

12

Miracles, speaking engagements, and extensive Internet experience in web development, software integration, and marketing.

Tracy specializes in online marketing campaigns that build a cohesive corporate or personal brand, using an integrated web strategy that helps you attract more leads, get more clients, and make more sales. Her solutions are done with marketing and results in mind. In addition, she has appeared as a technology specialist in National TV segments with *ABC7, San Diego Living, Good Morning New Mexico, CNBC, 4 Your Money, Report on Business, HGTV, FOX, ABC, NBC, KMIR, Life Love's Shopping, Daytime, Fox 5 Las Vegas, New Mexico Style, Vegas Inc, The CW, USA Today, Forbes, MSN Money, King5, CTV, CBS,* and over fifty publications, newspapers, and magazines, plus two motivational movies.

"Get Ready to Make an Instant Online Impact with a Fully Branded Complete End –to-End Website Presence and Message-to-Market System in Under 60 Days!"

To find out more about Tracy, visit http://www.TracyRepchuk.com

Visit Tracy's media page here:
http://www.TracyRepchukMedia.com

Visit Tracy's speaker booking page here:
http://www.TracyRepchukLive.com

Chapter 2

Speaking and Engaging Your Audience for the Ultimate Impact
by Gary Stuart

We all desire success. Whether it's in the competitive business world or simply within our own personal lives, we all hope to be the best we can be. Yet far too often, we feel at a loss as to how to attain the level of success we know we deserve. So often we feel we are at the effect of outside forces rather than in control of our own destiny.

Believe me, no one could have felt less in control of his life than I did. I was a child of poverty, of physical abuse, and my father died when I was very young. It seemed that my past had given me so many negatives to focus on that I carried those feelings of failure with me well into my adulthood. But then I discovered a way to view the past much differently than I ever had before. I discovered a modality known as Constellation work, and it has changed my life forever.

Now I am honored to share with you the steps I took those many years ago on my journey from ultimate victim to ultimate success. Ironically, that hadn't even been my goal. I had simply hoped to find happiness in spite of the odds being stacked against me. But soon I began to realize more than just

15

a sense of well-being. I began to realize my role in keeping myself stuck in a cycle of failure and subtle self-sabotage. And I realized that it was up to me to decide where my past ends and the present moment begins.

As a fully-accredited, double-certified Constellation facilitator for nearly two decades now, I have learned many valuable lessons on how to go from self-sabotaging to self-actualizing. You see, there are certain patterns of behavior we continue to repeat even though doing so may not serve us, not to mention patterns of thought which can hinder us as well. Yet there are some simple, pro-active steps you can take to help you not only recognize such patterns but empower you to break them. In other words, before you can move forward, you need to look back.

Step 1. Consider Your Connection to the Past

It's amazing how often people will expect to get a different result even though they don't take different action. We all make mistakes. We all fail to live up to our own expectations now and then. But what makes someone successful is the ability to learn from those mistakes, and to see what a gift such experiences truly are.

These allegedly negative events can actually strengthen our resolve and afford us the opportunity to develop problem-solving skills we would never otherwise have. For years I was so trapped in my own "coulda, shoulda, woulda" mindset that I was failing to see that I could harness the same energy I was expending by wallowing in *"what wasn't,"* and use it to work toward *"what can be."* In other words, I realized that being stuck in a rut of dissatisfaction was a choice. And I was ready to choose something different.

As I began to take stock of my personal and professional experiences, I began to see that the past had a greater impact on me than I had realized. It's not just my past, but my family's past too. I discovered that along with our family history, we also inherit an emotional blueprint from our ancestors which affects how we deal with the various challenges we face in our lives. Often there is an unspoken loyalty to those who came before, and a feeling that it is up to us to right their wrongs, or at the very least to limit our success so as not to bypass theirs.

These subconscious connections are known as entanglements, and they affect us much more than we realize. We all come from families whose habits and patterns may have developed as a reaction to a time and situation that no longer exists. Yet out of love and loyalty, we tend to mimic their perspectives and perpetuate their reactions even though doing so may not be serving us and, in fact, may be sabotaging our success.

But how do we break the pattern? How do we reconcile the guilt we may feel if we dare to be prosperous when they were not? And how can we overcome this fear of betrayal that keeps us from taking matters into our own hands? Believe it or not, the answer lies in acceptance.

Step 2. Transform Your Perception of The Past

As the old adage goes, *"Those who don't learn from the past are doomed to repeat it."* If I've learned one thing from my sixty-plus years on this Earth, it's just how very true this is. And when we consider how much we are shaped by not only our own experiences but by our familial examples as well, it's all the more important that we recognize just what a gift those experiences have been.

The worst thing we could do is to try and simply push the past away. When we say, *"I'm nothing like my mother,"* or *"I'll never be like my father,"* we are actually denying ourselves a very necessary and empowering connection to our creators. Even if we don't think of our family as a source of support, they still are. We wouldn't be here without them. And when we exclude them, we exclude a part of ourselves.

Empowerment requires wholeness. That's why every facet needs to be seen and included—the good, the bad, and the ugly. In order for us to break a pattern, we must first be willing to acknowledge its existence. Only then can we make the conscious choice to do things differently.

When I set out on my own healing path at a young age, I had no idea I was actually on my way to becoming a healing practitioner. My only intention was to heal myself. I wanted to grow and learn as much about my own internal process as I possibly could. In hindsight, I realize I was already developing the personal empowerment techniques I use and share today in my lectures and Constellation workshops. We are all being guided by forces larger than ourselves. I see now that my past experiences were actually the fodder for my yet unrealized future. Still, I would never know the level of empowerment or support I feel from my past if I hadn't chosen to change my negative perception of it.

The gift of choice is yours, so use it wisely. Stop and look at the choices you make, and consider what drives those decisions. Think before you act. And above all, don't just react. As we saw with the past, obstacles and challenges are teaching tools. Stop and think of the possible outcomes before you implement any changes so that you can be empowered by your own objectivity. The world actually encourages us more than we realize. And with each step comes another gift. The question is, are we open to receiving them?

Again, the gift of the past is experience, both our own as well as that of others. The gift of the present is choice: do we let the past entangle us or support us in moving forward? Remember, when we can come from a place of acceptance rather than rejection, then we are finally free to make those different choices that will lead to different results.

Step 3. Be Willing to Leave it in the Past

Obviously, our connections to the past are strong, but patterns can be broken and perceptions can be altered. When we are feeling stuck or at a loss as to how to proceed, we are actually demonstrating our loyalty to our established mode of operation. It's scary to try something new. And who would we be if we dared to do it differently?

But comfort zones only serve to limit our chances for greater success. We need to let go of what doesn't work in order to make room for what will.

The Constellation process helps us pinpoint the specific aspects with which we are entangled and need to disengage from (or better still, transform into support) in order to move forward. Having walked the talk, as they say, I know the process inside out and outside in, and I can help guide you along every liberating step of the way.

It is seeing these dynamics from a different perspective that allows us to understand the deeper truths about what may be blocking us from greater success. Once we are made aware of them, they can no longer exert their power in unseen ways, freeing us from any energetic hold they may have had. Simply put, the work brings objectivity to our subjective beliefs.

We all take on burdens that are not actually ours to carry. Constellations can help us distinguish what is and what isn't ours. They afford us the opportunity to harness the power of the past in new and empowering ways. And they make visible those previously unseen dynamics that have been adversely affecting our ability to move forward, personally or professionally.

Furthermore, we come away with a conscience free of guilt or shame, for we attain a deeper understanding that we share the same dream of prosperity and fulfillment with those who came before. And when it comes true for us, it comes true for them. But we do not need to carry anything for them. Their fate was theirs, and they can carry it. When we acknowledge their strength, we can acknowledge our own.

The road to success doesn't have to be a long and winding one. There are simple yet profound steps you can take to help you move forward into a prosperous and unencumbered future. Learn from your experiences. See that even the most negative ones still hold valuable lessons. And be willing to disentangle yourself from old patterns of thought or behavior that don't serve you.

It's your future. Let it come with the gift of empowerment. Take control of your own destiny, and shape it however you see fit, both personally and professionally.

You deserve success. You deserve happiness. You can have them both. I can show you how.

C⊚nstellation Healing
Institute ...with *Gary Stuart*

"Moving YOU Out of Your Past So YOU can Transform Your Future"

Gary's Special Offer:

I'd love to invite you to join my community and connect with me personally. There you will find a copy of my free gift:

5 Easy Steps to Propel You Out of Your Past and Make Your Transformation Now

I tune into the deeper dynamics as we speak and see what needs to be done to help you get to the place you want to be.

IMAGINE the RELIEF you'll feel when you're no longer STUCK! You'll begin to see things that were once negative in a more positive, empowering light.

Let's get you into the new winning framework, and above all, feel good doing it. It's the NOT CHANGING that creates suffering. Call or email me to book an appointment to set up your time for a free *"Discovery Call."* This alone will catapult you forward into the next level of success in your life. You deserve happiness and success on every level now! Is your past HOLDING YOU BACK? The time to start is NOW! To join my community and get your free gift go here:

http://www.HealingInActionNow.com

About Gary Stuart

Gary Stuart is a dedicated and spirited Constellation facilitator for fifteen plus years. Now double-certified, his first certification was completed during Heinz Stark's first U.S. facilitator training in 2000-2002. While continuing his weekly workshops, Gary then completed Bert Hellinger's first "Movements of the Spirit-Mind" training in Pichl, Austria in 2007 and certified in 2008.

Having facilitated well over 6,000 processes, Gary is now on the cutting edge applying the modality to prosperity, organizational empowerment and familial epigenetics, plus past-life re-incarnation issues. He continues to conduct weekly workshops in Los Angeles and other US cities. Gary also offers Distance Constellation healing work for personal, business, or organizational issues as well. He's created a comprehensive, Constellation Facilitator Mastery & Empowerment Workshop for Constellation Facilitators and other Therapists with his innovative instructional workbook.

He founded the Constellation Healing Institute, Inc. (C.H.I.) in 2008, and is the author of *Many Hearts, ONE SOUL*, which speaks to the spiritual aspects behind the modality of systemic constellation work. His innovative presentations at the 2011 and 2013 US Constellation conferences in San Francisco and Seattle were highly rated. He always WOWs all in attendance with an interactive, enlightening, unforgettable experience.

**To find out more about Gary, visit
http://www. ConstellationHealingInstitute.com**

Chapter 3

Consistency: A 7-Step Blueprint for Success in Selling You
by Bruce Keith

A few years ago I was having lunch with a friend who built up a very successful business as a professional salesperson. He asked me an interesting question, *"Bruce, you've been in sales a long time, plus you've helped thousands of other salespeople be successful with your personal coaching and seminars. What would you say is the most consistent challenge that salespeople are confronted with? What's the toughest thing they have to overcome?"*

I gave him a simple one-word answer . . . *consistency.* He replied, *"No, you don't understand, that's my question . . . what is the most consistent problem every salesperson has?"*

I laughed and said, *"The answer is in your question. The most common challenge all salespeople face is to maintain consistency in their performance—day after day after day. The biggest Achilles' heel that everyone struggles with is a lack of consistency."*

We both chuckled at this point because it looked like we were headed down a path similar to that of Abbott and Costello in their famous "Who's on first?" baseball skit. Once we got

23

back on track, we both agreed that this consistency issue is very beatable. There is absolutely no need for a lack of consistency to have any power over those determined to defeat it.

Being consistent will change your life! Many years ago, when I learned how to be consistent, it became one of the most valuable accomplishments in my business. It changed everything. Consistency will change your confidence level, it will change your mindset, it will change your income, and it will positively impact those around you. What follows is a very clear nine-step roadmap of how to make that happen for yourself.

The Concept of Consistency

Here is a bottom line truism . . . if you are consistent in your day-to-day performance, you will achieve great success. The opposite creates disaster. It's very black and white. Consistency equals success. Consistency is the result of doing the right things at the right time every day. Inconsistency comes from not doing the right things at the right time every day.

The concept of consistency is very simple: think of your business like a conveyor belt. Your conveyor belt is your "sales cycle." Let's use an example of a business where the conveyor belt is ninety days long from start to finish. What you do today shows up as a paycheck at the other end of the conveyor belt in approximately ninety days. Your job is to "load things on the conveyor belt" every single day and not allow any "gaps" in that conveyor belt. The price of being inconsistent is that a gap inevitably shows up at the other end. That gap translates into zero cash flow—not acceptable and clearly not what you had in mind when you got started, correct?

24

Here are nine proven ideas to eliminate those gaps. Start implementing these ideas and the dreaded inconsistency goes away. Your cash flow will improve dramatically—no more financial ups and downs. *Consistency* will become your middle name!

Idea 1: Be Crystal Clear on Where You're Going

High production is never a problem for those who have clear and specific goals. Constantly reviewing your personal motivation is the key to a consistent performance. This will help you fight off those nasty interruptions that are always coming up. There are two parts to this very critical issue:

1.   *Do I know what I want?*

2.   *Do I always keep my goals top of mind?*

Let's look at them individually.

Do I know what I want?

Many salespeople tell me they have a very clear picture of what they want . . . *"It's in my head, Bruce.".* The experts have proven over and over that if it's not written down or displayed on a dream board, then it's not clear enough! You should have a minimum of five to six specific goals that identify exactly why you are doing all the things you need to be doing. A simple approach is to identify two goals for your health, two for your family/social, and two for your financial future. Each one should exhibit the following three characteristics: they must be specific, measurable, and time dependent. For example, if you wanted to take your family to Disneyland then your goal would look like this . . . *"I am taking my whole family (all four of us) to Disneyland in March at a cost of $5,200. We will be flying there and staying for five days at the Marriott Hotel."*

Do I always keep my goals top of mind?

Keep your goals top of mind. It's one thing to have your goals identified but there's no point in putting them in a desk drawer and leaving them there. As retired NCAA Coach Woody Hayes said, *"Hope is not a strategy."* Your goals must be highly visible and you should literally review them every single day. For example, they could be on a vision board for you to look at every morning.

Another suggestion is to write them out at least once a week and read them out loud daily. Science has proven that there is a powerful connection between the paper, the pen, your hand, your arm, and your brain. This definitely helps reinforce your determination to make it all happen.

Everyone knows the above information is valid—very few people do it. If you want to create consistency in your life and your business, you've got to be motivated, especially on those days you don't feel like it! Stay motivated, be ever conscious of "where I'm going," and you will be much more consistent.

Idea 2: Know Your Results at All Times

Keeping track of your numbers is critical if you want to succeed. You wouldn't play golf without keeping score, would you? You wouldn't enter a weight-loss contest without getting on the scale periodically, would you? The whole idea of keeping track is to compare where you are now with where you want to end up, i.e. your goal for the week, month, or year. There are three main components you must track at all times. They are:

1. *Am I making enough contacts?*

2. *Am I going on enough appointments?*

3. *Am I making enough sales?*

Now here's the best part: once you keep track, you can make adjustments as you go. This will guarantee you will get to your final destination as planned. It's like driving a car; if you start to veer off the road you make an adjustment to keep going in the right direction. Making adjustments along the way is the icing on the cake for your business. This is all part of the result your consistency provides.

Idea 3: Assume One Hundred Percent Responsibility for Your Success

It doesn't matter where you work or the size of your market, or even your experience in sales. If you do what you're supposed to do you will achieve the goals you have set. It's never too late to start the journey. It's never too late to change the direction of the journey you are on.

Start by taking on this mindset: assume that you are one hundred percent in charge of how successful you are going to be. The 80/20 rule is a safe assumption no matter what your business and no matter what your marketplace is like right now. It says that eighty percent of the income is being earned by twenty percent of the selling population. Your job is to make sure you are part of the twenty percent. It's easy to look at the other eighty percent of the population who aren't making much money and understand why they are in that group. The reality is it's not the market . . . it's them. They're not consistent. The twenty percent of the sales force are doing the right things and are doing them consistently.

They make all the money. The people that are not making enough money always have excuses and stories as to why *"It's not my fault."* Here are two guidelines for you to follow:

1. Associate with the twenty percent. Find out what they're doing and do the identical activities all the time. In other words, match their activities and do it consistently.

2. Stay away from the eighty percent group. They will infect your mind and reduce your ability to fight off adversity and interruptions. They are always looking for reasons why they aren't succeeding and they never hesitate to share them with everyone. Stay away!

Idea 4 : Understand the "Power of NEXT"

Everybody experiences a periodic slump or a setback in their business. The key is to get over it quickly! The Power of NEXT says that no matter what is going on, move forward. Tony Robbins shares a great expression that says, *"There is a reason why the rearview mirror is so much smaller than the windshield."* Don't look back. Don't panic when things go wrong. Part of being mentally tough is dealing with adversity. It's all about who you are in the tough times, not just the good times.

It's very normal in business for you to be subjected to fluctuations in market circumstances, ongoing rejection, and the unpredictability of the people you deal with. When you experience a setback, get in the habit of saying NEXT, and move forward. Those that are inconsistent will typically fall prey to drama and consequently they do not perform the task at hand as originally planned. They get off track and the result is disastrous. Sometimes a whole day or more is lost.

Employing the "NEXT technique" for staying consistent is difficult for a lot of people. They see others getting off track for all the wrong reasons but when something happens to them they justify the drama by saying things like, "*You don't understand, this is different.*" It isn't different . . . that's just their story!

Being consistent requires you to get over it quickly and move on. Make NEXT your favorite four letter word.

Idea 5: Start Every Day at Zero

Here's a simple plan to really stay consistent. First of all, learn to start every day at zero; assume you have no leads, no hot prospects, no sales, and nothing pending. Now, set a minimum standard for what you intend to accomplish each day and stick to that commitment. Think about how your business runs best. It could be to make at least twenty contacts per day; it could be to set a minimum of one appointment per day; it could be to ask for referrals from everyone you speak to.

Your job is to first set those minimum standards and follow them every single day. NO Excuses.

When you take this approach it helps you jump out of bed every morning with the right attitude. Your mind says "*I've got a great day ahead of me and I know exactly what I have to do.*" Those that are inconsistent don't take this approach; they don't set a minimum standard and as a result they're always in "react mode." React Mode says, "*I'm going to do whatever*

29

comes up because I have nothing planned and it's not my fault if things don't go right." Here's how the inconsistent salesperson justifies being in react mode. They say, *"It's not like I'm not working. I'm really busy—seems like I'm working seven days a week right now. I can only do so much in twenty-four hours you know!"* The sad truth is that this is just more proof that busywork isn't necessarily productive work.

When you start every day at zero, you are not resting on your laurels. Everything you do is aimed at what's coming up versus what happened yesterday. One last thought for this point: don't set up a huge "to do list" for yourself every day. Keep your minimum standards short and sweet. Starting every day at zero doesn't mean you take on a huge list of new tasks. It simply means you assume responsibility for the things that have to be done first.

Idea 6: Protect Your Self-Confidence

One of the biggest drawbacks to staying consistent is a fluctuation in your self confidence.

There is a reason why commissioned sales is one of the highest price paid professions in the world. It's a tough job. Sales can be a lonely business.

Often, you're on your own and it's up to you to stay strong. Having strong self-confidence is a critical part of staying consistent.

Guard your self-confidence with the highest level of commitment. When things go wrong, when there are setbacks, many salespeople "beat themselves up." It shows up in self-defeating statements like, *"That was dumb"* or *"How could I have been so stupid?"* or *"Why didn't I say that when I had the chance?"*

These kinds of comments are tremendously detrimental to maintaining a high level of self-confidence. Consider that every time you beat yourself up, you are eroding your self-confidence. There is absolutely no value in self-abuse. When you do so, you are creating negative affirmations about yourself. Here are some great alternatives for you to use instead . . .

"I learn from my mistakes. I move forward in a positive way."

"I'm getting better and better every day."

"Negativity has disappeared from my life!"

"I'm so excited about the person I am becoming!"

You need to constantly remind yourself of your successes. There's nothing wrong with patting yourself on the back every once in a while. This doesn't mean your ego is out of control, it means you are celebrating your successes and then moving forward to take on new challenges. Just make sure to take the time to reinforce to yourself that the path you are on is the road to your ultimate success. Stay confident at all times!

7. Complacency is Always Around the Corner

Incredibly, many salespeople are guilty of "letting up just before the finish line." Don't try to figure out why; it just happens. The finish line can be defined very simply as the next target on the map. The finish line could be the end of the day, the end of the week, or even the end of the month. Complacency usually shows up in two ways:

1. *"I've got a lot of good things on the go so I don't really need to load up the conveyor belt right now— I'm pretty busy as it is. I'll just wait until the sales come through. I'm in good shape!"*

2. *"It looks like I've got this all figured out now . . . my business pretty well happens the way it's supposed to. I've done the hard work so now I can reap the benefits without knocking myself out anymore."*

Both of these concepts are short-lived. The individuals who are highly successful never let up; they go right to the end, day after day after day. If they take time off—if they back off on their intensity—it's because it was planned time off that was part of their schedule, not just because they got lazy on the spur of the moment. Work all the time that you work and take time off to refresh yourself. Just make sure it's planned in advance.

Complacency is insidious—it's always there. If you're not careful it will come up and bite you when you least expect it. With that in mind, here's a final secret for going from good to great; when you get ahead of your goals do not let up, simply push forward and stay focused. This is where the danger of complacency is the strongest. Give it no power!

Idea 8: "Winging it" Doesn't Get the Job Done

Here's a hidden truth for you as we near the end of the list; it's much easier to be consistent when you have frequent success. The way to have frequent success is to constantly be improving your sales skills. The only way to improve your skills is to do what every other top professional does—constantly practice. This is the opposite of "winging it."

32

Winners practice, losers don't. Consistency in your sales delivery comes from knowing what to say, how to say it, and saying it naturally. The problem is, often "natural isn't natural." What I mean is that it takes time to perfect using all the "right words" and having them flow as part of your conversation, so it really sounds like you. It is the same for every profession; it requires a commitment to excellence. The biggest difference by far in creating consistent success is setting aside the *time to practice.* If you want a guaranteed success formula, then do this: make sure you are practicing your scripts and dialogs (with role-play partners and/or yourself) for thirty minutes in the morning every single day.

This can be done. I have done it for years and dozens of my coaching clients are doing the same right now. You have to put it in your schedule and make it happen (remember, if it isn't in your schedule, it doesn't get done).

Here's a sobering truth; very few people take this advice and actually practice every day. There is always an excuse or a reason why it doesn't work for them.

Like anything else however, if others can do it, so can you. If you really want to be different, if you really want to stand out, then this is a guaranteed strategy.

Learn what to say and then practice how to say it over and over. The alternative is to "wing it." Winging it is all part of that definition of insanity, *"Doing the same thing over and over and expecting different results."* The reason this greatly impacts your consistency is because your results will suffer and consequently so will your desire to overachieve. It's much easier to be successful when you have frequent wins along the way. You can practice regularly, many people do. It works incredibly well. You must decide on your own on this one.

Observation: obviously some of these techniques are easier than others. This may be the toughest one of all. It also

33

pays off in huge increments! Don't let the power of practice escape you. The cost of not doing so and "winging it" is to stay the same and not get any better at the most critical part of selling—the skill of communication.

Idea 9: Stay Away from Shortcuts

Avoid all temptation to look for shortcuts. Your challenges are usually pretty predictable; your business and your life are made up of a series of problems that need to be solved. Remember Beverly Sills' great quote, *"There are no shortcuts to any place worth going."* A common shortcut salespeople often take is not talking to enough new prospects each day. Let's look at two more.

Not Asking Enough Questions

Another example of taking a shortcut is not asking enough questions in the sales process. It usually shows up when you close too soon. When you offer the solution to a prospect before you are really clear on what they need and want, you are taking a dangerous shortcut. It would be like a doctor prescribing the wrong medicine before identifying the illness first. Don't fall into that trap.

Not Showing Added Value

Another place that shortcuts can show up is in the actual sales presentation. Too many salespeople do not do an effective job of showing their prospects the critical added value that they are bringing to the table. They don't really demonstrate the all-important "I am different." When that happens, you are not allowing the prospect to see the advantages you offer over the competition. This makes it difficult for them to see why they should choose you. A second downside to that shortcut is that the prospect starts to say "*No*" before they really understand why you are the best choice. This makes it even tougher. It's a difficult mentality to turn around after it starts.

Consider this critical part of being consistent; there is always a formula for getting things done the right way. When you are inconsistent in following that formula—meaning taking shortcuts—what ends up happening is your results become inconsistent. If you were training for a marathon you would follow a very straightforward regimen that tells you what to eat, how much, and how much training to do to build up your strength. Not doing so results in poor performance.

It's the same in your sales business. Plain and simple: you can't afford to take shortcuts!

BONUS Idea:
Write Out Your Top Three Every Morning

Being consistent means getting it done every day. The definition of "it" in this case is to always focus on your top priorities. It is critical that first thing every morning, you identify those three top priorities. Take the time to sit down and identify your top three and write them out. Don't just say "*I've got them in my head, I know what they are.*" Write them on a piece of paper and keep it with you all day. This will help you put a "red flag" on what's really important so that you don't forget what has to be done. Your commitment is simply this: no matter what else falls by the wayside, these three items must be completed.

Your job is to make sure you complete those three tasks before your day is done, no matter how long it takes. Consider this truth: if they are your top priorities, then nothing else

35

should get in the way. Every day, be very clear what you have to complete before you are finished. Make sure these three items are top of your list each day.

This is not easy to do all the time. Many salespeople are guilty of not saying *"No"* often enough. Warren Buffett said that the single most contributing factor to his success was his ability to say *"No."* He is famous for saying that, *"I say NO to ninety-nine percent of the things that come my way each day."* While this ninety-nine percent is probably not realistic for your business, by having your top three front and center, it makes it much easier for you to decide how you're going to spend your time. Put it in your routine to write them out first thing every day . . . and then follow through.

Wrapping Up

Now you know what it takes to be *consistent.* The next step is to start implementing. It's one thing to know what to do, it's another thing to do something about it. As Jim Rohn said, *"Knowledge without labor is useless."*

Here's a very effective implementation plan so you can get started. . .

You don't have to take on all of the above techniques right away. Do them one at a time and create an accumulation effect. Your momentum will gain power rapidly as your consistency builds. Take on just one of these ideas every single week for the next ten weeks. Pick the one for this week that appeals to you the most. Pick one you know you can start right away. Put that in place and make sure it is part of "the new you" every single day of the first week. Next week take on the second item and put it in place. Just make sure you don't interrupt the consistency of the first item. It becomes cumulative. The momentum you will create is incredibly powerful! Week #3, week #4, week #5, and so forth.

Within six to eight weeks you will become incredibly consistent! The exciting thing is you will never look back. These techniques will become part of who you are. Now you have a new middle name . . . CONSISTENCY. Good luck, this program will transform your results in an amazing way. Your business will never be the same!

Bruce's Special Offer:

As a highly respected business and sales coach, Bruce Keith has a record of helping thousands dramatically enhance their business results in a short period of time. The successes enjoyed by Bruce's clients are the result of two very solid approaches to "helping you build your business":

#1. A very personalized coaching style focusing on your strengths and not your weaknesses. Bruce's clients typically report the following . . . *"First he understood who I am and then he helped me build a plan complete with the necessary action steps that took my business to a whole new level."*

#2. Ongoing accountability to make sure you stay on track and do the things that need to be done. Bruce takes a *NO Excuses* line . . . *"He worked with me to get past the 'I know what to do, I've just got to do it' roadblock and then my results really took off. Bruce is amazing!"*

If you want to be the person "you know you can be," go to **http://BruceKeithResults.com** to find out more. No long-term contracts, no fluff . . . a personal approach that gets results!

About Bruce Keith

Bruce Keith is a leading trainer for sales organizations in North America. Bruce was exceptionally well trained in the corporate world as a marketing and sales manager for fifteen years with IBM. He's spent the last twenty-five plus years in the real estate industry; the first ten of those as a highly successful real estate salesperson, and the last fifteen years as an acclaimed keynote speaker, seminar leader, author, and one-on-one coach.

Bruce has worked with many multinational organizations such as Freedom 55/London Life, Remax, Century 21, Keller Williams, Weichert, Coldwell-Banker, and TD Waterhouse. His high energy coupled with a *"No Excuses Accountability"* approach has helped thousands increase their production significantly. As Bruce says, *"A great coach is someone who will not let you settle for what you think is your best."*

An entertaining speaker, Bruce takes a down-to-earth approach using stories, real-life examples, and humor to communicate and interact very effectively with his audiences. His "no fluff" style ensures that *"Everyone leaves with specific action steps on how to transform their business permanently."*

As a contributing author, Bruce's articles and blogs appear frequently in publications such as REM—the Real Estate Magazine, Re/Max Best Agent, and IXACT Contact. His *Sales Assist Products* address a broad range of the business of sales.

To find out more about Bruce, visit http://BruceKeithResults.com

Chapter 4

7 Secrets to Being
Happy and Successful in Business
by Vivian De Guzman

A lot of people come to me due to aches and pain they thought were purely physical, and through my intuitive and detailed assessment, I am able to get to the root cause of the problem whether it is physical, emotional, mental, psychological, psychic (other people's energies) or spiritual.

My goal is to bridge spirituality and the physical world so people can understand how to be happy while pursuing their goals and dreams. This is applicable in health, money, and relationships as they are all interconnected.

I started out as a holistic PT (physical therapist) treating cancer patients, then switched markets to help women business owners get fast, positive results in business/money, health, and relationships. Initially, I was looking to make money, however (as every business owner knows), you are often stretched beyond your comfort zone to discover the highest version of you. When you are searching for yourself, you're basically looking for soul enlightenment, and once you take that path outside traditional medicine, you're telling God/Universe to show you where your flaws are, and what to

41

do, or where to go to get to enlightenment. Divine Source shows you all the difficult situations and people you need to deal with; it's like polishing a diamond, you have to go through the fire to look nice and pretty.

What made me clear on what I wanted was that I basically got everything I didn't want, so I figured out what I truly wanted. For five years, my private practice became my training wheels on how to build a successful business. It boiled down to learning how to love, honor, and respect myself unconditionally, which meant really knowing who I was without the money conversations of my parents and ancestors, meaning. . . I had to release any limiting subconscious beliefs that were holding me back, in order to become successful. It meant letting go of my judgments about rich people (because I was given the wrong scripting about them), and redefining how I wanted myself to think, do, and feel when I became rich. It meant redefining what wealth means to me and redefining my most important values and principles.

How did I get to six figures in six months of launching my new business? Here are the steps I've been doing that help me feel happy and successful every day.

Seven Basic Steps to Feeling Happy and Successful Every Day

1. How to Practice Receiving

I set aside a "me time" in my *intentional schedule* every day for self care, such as daily clearing of my energy, doing deep breathing, nature walks, massage, acupuncture, hot yoga, and anything else that nourishes my soul. This is essential in order to receive and balance out what I give. I also realize that

42

when my energy is clear, my ideal clients find me easily and effortlessly.

Always feel good before you do anything. In fact, I don't go downstairs and greet my family until I feel balanced and grounded. This way, my family sees me in my best self and best behavior. Ever since I started doing this, I have drastically reduced sickness in my family.

2. How to Stay in Alignment

I clarified my values (my top three are freedom, integrity, and authenticity) and live them every day. When things are rocky, I always go back to check if any of my values are being violated and then I correct the action based on my values. My energy clearing technique to really stay in alignment is clearing all my chakras daily, to make sure that what I think and feel, match up.

3. What I Do When the Going Gets Tough

I do daily meditation to get Divine messages from God/Divine Source, having complete trust and faith for the instructions given.

I do active meditation (written conversations with God) when I have challenges in business. For example, in 2014, I was told to follow Lisa Sasevich's formula in doing teleclinics, private sessions, and retreats/events. This year (2015), I was guided to do out-of-the-country retreats and get clients through speaking and private sessions, and to build my Transformational Wellness Academy and my online presence. Teleclinics are not to be repeated so I am on a new path with complete trust as to what is going to unfold. Actually, I tried to put together a teleclinic, and offered it in December and

January, however it's interesting that even though it's a new topic, it didn't sell. Again, that's my *brain* working, because I made about $20,000 last year just on teleclinics, but that's not what my Divine guides are telling me, so I will redirect my efforts in the next few months.

4. How to Have Unlimited Abundance

I write in my gratitude journal—every morning—ten things I am grateful for. At night, I go back to it and write with notes of success (what did I do today that made me feel successful?).

5. How to Be Successful

I plan the structure of my business and work backwards to implement the results, along with a mentor who understands me, my dreams, and my goals. I chose Tracy Repchuk as my mentor this year. To me, completely trusting in my Divine guidance helps me move forward even though people around me say don't.

6. Mantra to Help Me in Sales

My favorite saying is, *"What if you could never fail, what would you do today?"* This has been my guiding principle when I make phone calls to connect with potential clients; former and current clients; and even potential partners.

7. How to Have Consistent Money Flow

Paying myself first and saving money, along with designing my sales funnel and writing down my income daily on my calendar has helped me stay financially stable. This provides the container for making and receiving the money. Without this, I noticed I was spinning my wheels and it didn't matter how much money I made, because it would just go to expenses. Journaling how much income I had focused my attention on the income rather than the expenses.

The Different Principles and Laws of Thought and the Universe I Follow Consciously

Principle #1

Thoughts are forces of energy that impact and shape our lives and reality. Follow the seventeen-second rule.

Result

Life no longer happens to you, instead you can create the life you want.

A thought that is weak and scattered has weak and scattered energy, consequently it will have little impact on your life. But a thought that is directed, concentrated, and repeated over and over again on a regular basis becomes a powerful force—much like a belief, and this kind of thought will shape and impact your life.

For example, if you think that when you get old, you'll have lots of sickness, then that will be your reality. Do you know that the only reason older people have aches and pains is because they do not let go of certain habits that do not support their health? Let's take a look. How many old people have constant worries, fears, eat unhealthy foods (because they say "*I can eat whatever I want, I'm already old*"), or follow certain traditions without questioning whether they still support them or not (because that's what they're used to)? How is it that there are older people who are very active, always happy, and socializing with other peers, even playing sports with   other people? When you sit down and talk to them, they don't usually talk about their aches and pains, but their plans . . . what they are going to do next. That's the kind of mentality I want to have!

Principle #2

The mind is constantly sending and receiving thoughts.

Result

You'll learn how to prioritize your actions based on what you decide is important to you.

We're not immune to other people's thoughts. They travel and have an impact on us. That's why, for example, you may be thinking of a former high school classmate, then the phone rings and it's her. This usually happens to the people close to you; you may be thinking about going to a particular restaurant when your friend says, *"I was just thinking about the same thing!"* This is your subconscious mind picking up on their thoughts and sending them to your subconscious mind where you act on them.

Most business owners love to think. In fact, they have multiple ideas streaming through their head at any given moment in time, and yet only a few things are accomplished due to a lack of focus and clarity. Another reason why this is happening is related to how your chakras/energy centers are moving and if they are in alignment. A thought comes to us through the top of our head—normally on the eighth or ninth chakra—and once we catch that thought, it has to be processed down through our other chakras for it to manifest into reality. When we start thinking more about it, such as how to go about executing the plan, that is all happening in the seventh chakra. Then we start seeing evidence of it through our sixth chakra/third eye, when we can see the end result of our thought. Then we talk about it through our fourth chakra/throat. Then we start to really feel it through our heart chakra. We get empowered to move in the direction of accomplishing that thought. Sometimes, women business owners get derailed because of their emotions/second chakra. If everything feels good and things are lining up, we can manifest it into reality through our first chakra. Then we receive the money for it.

That's the mechanical explanation of how thoughts become realities all the way to receiving the money. However, if you have doubts, limiting beliefs, fears, or lack of resources, you start to look the other way and stall the process. When your chakras are not spinning properly or if they're not moving at all, you tend to have physical and emotional problems as well.

You see, if everybody knows how the energy centers work, they would not hesitate doing the next best thing.

Principle #3

You will only find God in silence.

Result

You can use the energy that created the world to produce ten times the result of pure action alone.

Masters meditate. Millionaires meditate. Successful and powerful people meditate. Monks and priests meditate. Why? Because when you offer action items, you are literally using your physical energy to get what you want. When you start taking care of yourself and connecting with Divine Source/Higher Power, you will get Divine downloads/messages that speak volumes on what you need to do for the day or for a particular project. You'll learn the importance of having faith and trust even if you can't see the steps.

I did this in 2014 after I dropped my PT practice. I was doing active meditation—conversing with God on paper—and I was given specific instructions to attend a specific event and listen to the speaker, and follow her formula for the whole year: teleclinic, private sessions, and retreats/events. I even got the specific days and months I should be doing the retreats and how many times that year. On my first retreat, nine people showed up and we sold $29,000 worth of products and services that three-day weekend. I was stunned! I realized I just need to have faith and God will bring the rest to me. This got me inspired. Did I follow His instructions to the T? Of course not! I squeezed in two extra retreats which were not very successful monetarily, although I still justified it as successful, as I learned specific things I need to do to improve my speaking ability, my planning skills, my marketing strategy, and more! By the time 2014 arrived, I realized that when I'm doing my soul purpose, I am no longer in blame-mode with my mentors and coaches. I now own my decisions and I learn from my mistakes. With this, comes the next principle I applied.

Principle #4

Law of attraction: thoughts that are packed with emotion become magnetized and attract similar thoughts.

Result

Knowing that your emotions fuel your thoughts heightens your awareness so you can change the reality you are living.

If you're thinking of a thought, it only takes seventeen seconds for the Universe to match it up with a similar thought. For example, if you have a new desire to make more money and you hold that for seventeen seconds (meaning you're thinking about it or ways on how to do it) then the Universe matches you up with it. If your next thought is in conflict with your first one, then the second thought cancels out the first thought. Therefore one key to manifest what you desire consistently is to be focused, clear, and consistent with that thought.

What happens when you're angry? That is an outward energy needing to be released, therefore if you stay angry, most likely you'll find customers cancelling on you or your deals not closing. Observe your pattern, and if you see this happening, shift immediately by putting your palm on your pelvic region below the belly button and move it clockwise (right to left direction, forming a circle). Remember you only have seventeen seconds for the Universe to match this feeling with another thought, so shift from angry to calm fast!

Principle #5

Law of control: we are always experiencing thoughts but we have the ability to keep these thoughts or get rid of them.

Result

You will learn how to value your time and undo bad habits such as food addiction/emotional eating; being a shopaholic even if you don't need to buy; and other destructive or negative patterns that reflect self-sabotage.

This is very evident when a person has much clutter in their house or office. Sometimes we use this to distract ourselves from focusing on what's really important to us. I advocate decluttering your physical environment in addition to decluttering your mind through deep breathing, meditation, or nature walks. In fact, I don't start my day or any project until I feel clear, balanced and centered.

To help me with this, I had to redefine what "exercise" means to me. Back in 1998-2011, my health started deteriorating and I could no longer do my step aerobics or even the elliptical machine without getting short of breath. I wasn't overweight, however I just felt winded every time I did it. Or, my energy would go up during the exercise, leaving me feeling exhausted for at least two hours afterwards. To help me get back to my consistent exercise, I promised myself I would exercise every day for thirty days. Knowing I am an over-achiever, I decided to redefine exercise as something I do for myself for at least five minutes a day, which meant deep breathing would be classified as an exercise, or walking, or doing arm or leg exercises. On the sixth or seventh day (a weekend), I started getting lazy, and had to do my self-talk because I committed to myself (and no one else) in writing that I would exercise for thirty days. So, I continued with deep breathing or some arm exercises to get over this hump, and after thirty days, I checked it off—and I was so proud of myself when I was done! Then, my friend invited me to attend a hot yoga class, and I signed up for a two-week introductory program for only twenty dollars; from then on, I loved it so much that I continued with it three times a week until now. I realized that only I control my thoughts, and when there's consistency built in, I can accomplish any goal I want.

Principle #6

Law of insertion: we have the ability to insert any thought we want into our mind at anytime.

Result

You can shift your negative reality into positive reality in a matter of seconds.

One Tuesday morning, I was driving and I was stressed out about the upcoming $3,000 rent I had for my business, which was due that Friday. I realized that God/Universe always provides me with money when I need it, however, it's at the last minute! So, I've gone through these stressful months almost every single month, when it finally hit me that I have this pattern! I realized I was saying, *"Money comes to me easily and effortlessly"* however, I'm not specific on the date! When I got this, I started saying out loud while I was driving that Tuesday morning, *"Money comes to me WAY BEFORE I NEED IT."* I must have said that thirty times, or like I always tell my clients, *"Say it until you feel the shift* (like you really believe it's true!)." Do you know that another client bought a package for $1,200 *and* I received an unexpected check in the mail as a refund from the bank for $1,800 plus? Miracles do happen when you know how to apply the laws of thought and the Universe.

Principle #7

Law of connection: the inner world and the outer world are connected through our thoughts.

Result

When our conscious and subconscious mind are in alignment (meaning there is no conflict), we reap the rewards of positive affirmation.

I have done a lot of deep work in my soul by clearing multiple negative beliefs that I didn't know I had! Things like vows of poverty (we were middle class, not poor—even in the Philippines—so it must have come from my ancestors), financial self-sabotage, debt, family blocks, birth trauma, and other things that affect my money flow.

When I saw that the foundation of my business is *myself,* I realized I have to give myself the time to feel good, rejuvenate, eat healthy, exercise properly, sleep well, and think positive thoughts so I can share my gifts without resistance or hesitation to those who would like to experience them. I also had to repair the damages of my energetic boundaries, which allowed me to stay protected and connected in work, love, and life.

Transformational Wellness International
Master Your Natural Pathways to Healing ...with Vivian De Guzman

Vivian's Special Offer:

Get a FREE video course on
How to be a Money Magnet
Beyond the Law of Attraction

at **http://www.MoneyMagnetActivator.com**

For women business owners who are looking for
their soul purpose and highest version of themselves,
get your FREE copy of

Vivian's 7 Steps to Unleash Your Money Magnet
and Breakthrough Your Financial Ceiling NOW!

visit

A **http://www.yourfinancialbreakthrough.com**

About Vivian De Guzman

Vivian De Guzman is an international best-selling author, speaker, and the founder of Transformational Wellness Academy, and known as the #1 Money Magnet Activator. She is a fast transformational catalyst, licensed physical therapist, and a medical and business intuitive. An entrepreneur from age twenty-one, she started and sold two businesses while working full-time as a physical therapist and being a mother of four. In December 2013, she stepped into her soul purpose and mission of transforming people's lives and making them money magnets by "seeing" their obstacles. She helps clients, CEOs, and companies improve by clearing invisible negative energies so money and relationship flow easily.

Through the gift of "seeing," she visualizes the anatomy of the body and your energy field to help correct the problem, be it physical, emotional, mental, psychological, psychic, or spiritual. She's a Reiki Master, an Integrative Manual Therapy practitioner, a Chinese Energetics Medicine practitioner, and knows Theta Healing and Psychic Energetic Clearing. After thousands of cases, she realized healing occurs at a deep level, and when you get to the root of the problem, your health, money conversation, and relationships start to shift—so fast that you need support to embrace this new and higher version of self. She believes the most important person in your business is YOU. If you're aligned, your journey can be successful.

To find out more about Vivian, visit http://www.VivianDeGuzman.com

54

Chapter 5

Create Your Ultimate Business Lifestyle with Proven Systems and Strategies
by Shirley Dalton

If you're in business and working long, long hours and feeling tired, stressed out, and overwhelmed, what I call "Fed Up Freddy" or "Tired Out Terry," you most likely will want to argue the heading with me by saying, *"It's not possible. It can't be done."*

It is possible. It can be done and I am going to prove it to you.

In this chapter you're going to meet Paul, one of my favorite and most successful clients, who went from being a tired, exhausted, and frustrated business owner—who by his own account, thought he could last another twelve months before he either sold the business or just walked away from it—to owning an even more profitable business that runs very well without him.

You're going to learn the secrets to Paul's success. You're going to learn what Paul did and how he managed to reduce his contribution to the company revenue from three quarters of the entire company's revenue, down to just five percent whilst maintaining profitability.

And if you're anything like Paul, you'll be thinking you don't have the time to read this, let alone seek help. In fact, his colleague kept encouraging him, *"You have to meet Shirley." "Paul, talk to Shirley— she's the one person who understands your situation and the one person who can help you change it."*

On some level, Paul's subconscious must have known because after about six months of keeping in contact with me, he finally found the time to meet. At last, he accepted where he was at and asked for help.

That's one of the first and most important things any business owner can do. It's not a weakness to put your hand up and ask for help. If you knew how to fix it you'd already have fixed it. That's not your expertise, but it is mine. I've developed a five-step system that can help you create your ultimate business lifestyle. Keep reading and I'll share it with you.

Here's what I've found working with hundreds of business owners and entrepreneurs just like you; you go into business because you are good at what you do. You are a technician, a doer, and because you are so good at what you do, and generally good at sales and marketing, your business grows and grows and grows.

You come to realize you can't do it all yourself (even though you want to—you don't trust that others can do it as well as you). You reluctantly hire some people to help you. Suddenly you've become the leader and manager; responsible for recruiting, training, leading, managing, and holding your team accountable.

In most cases you've never been trained how to do this. You're a technician, good at what you do but not good at leading and managing people, and certainly not skilled or trained in running a business.

These skills can be learned. You just have to be willing and open to learn.

Fortunately for me, Paul proved to be a very keen student, although he didn't start out that way.

A very successful principal of a real estate agency, Paul had been working practically twenty-four hours a day, seven days a week for over fifteen years, and like most successful business owners, Paul began by telling me how I was going to solve his problem. I just smiled and ignored that.

"Shirley, I want to start with a plan. Let's create a business plan for where I want to go," he instructed.

Inwardly I was groaning.

"Yes Paul, we can do that, but how about we just start? Let's start with you," I suggested.

He frowned, *"What do you mean, start with me?"* he asked. *"In my experience Paul, having worked with hundreds of business owners, just like you, the first place to start is with the owner. The reason is simple, until you understand who you are and how you do things, you can't possibly expect to teach others and delegate to them, and that's exactly what you need to do, if you're going to free yourself from this trap you've created for yourself."* (See our online television program www.Untrapped.TV for inspirational stories, tips, and strategies for creating your ultimate business lifestyle.)

"But I want to get started," he said.

"I know, so do I, but let's get started with you first."

He was still not convinced about the need to be able to teach others and delegate (the *"No-one can do it as good as I can"* syndrome), so I pulled out the big guns.

"I wonder where your franchisor would be today if he had that belief and attitude; if he believed that no-one else could do it as well as he could?" I questioned.

Bingo.

He thought about how much he paid in franchise fees each year and how many hundreds of agencies did the same, all across the country.

"*Okay, let's go,*" he said.

For the next several months, Paul and I met regularly and together we worked on Paul.

He described me as Mary Poppins and I called him Action Jackson.

I carried a large bag with me to our meetings and he never quite knew what I was going to bring out of my bag (literally or figuratively), but somehow it always seemed to be the exact right tool, technique, activity, resource, or training. He often remarked about the insights I had and how valuable these were to him as he gained a greater sense of self-awareness.

And it wasn't long before I learned that I had to preface my words with "*Now we are just discussing this, this isn't a recommendation,*" because Paul would swing into action practically before the session was over.

Paul applied himself and began to understand the importance of knowing his people. He came to value training and empowering his team. He learned that most everyone comes to work to succeed and he became very motivated to multiply and clone his success as an agent. Not surprisingly, his team was equally keen to learn.

Paul ultimately realized that in order for his team to succeed, all he really needed to do was to "get out of their way and let them do it".

He was becoming a master of the first P in our triple P system. He had learned to lead and manage himself and others (*People*) because businesses aren't run by systems, they are run by people and you really can't have one without the other.

(If you're interested to learn how to lead and manage others, check out our programs on the "Work with Us" tab of www.ShirleyDalton.com).

Processes

Now that Paul had a handle on his people, it was time to focus on his systems and *Processes*.

Together we discovered and documented why and how he did what he did.

With this new awareness he was able to teach his team, and together they improved their results and productivity.

Paul also began to make better recruitment decisions because he was now clear about the roles and responsibilities within his business and was able to advertise for and qualify candidates who would fit his new culture.

Paul's team lifted to the point where his business started to grow and he went from being responsible for bringing in seventy-six percent of the total company revenue, down to five percent.

Without the constant burden of having to generate revenue, Paul now had time to think and to focus on other things. He started to work on his business and even allowed himself some free time, something he would never have done before. In fact, the first few times he took time off from work during work hours he felt like he was truanting from the business. He felt guilty. When he finally did allow himself to enjoy his much deserved freedom, he focused on improving his golf game and quickly reduced his handicap to zero.

Possibilities

Paul was ecstatic. He no longer had to do the doing. He promoted one of his team to Sales Manager and acquired a number of businesses as part of his expansion program (yes, we did eventually create his business plan).

The third P—*Possibility*, soon became *Probability* as Paul expanded his vision of what was possible and took action towards achieving his new goals.

Today Paul has huge plans for expansion and his free time includes travelling the world and sailing his motor cruiser with his wife.

Paul is a great example of what can happen when you focus on your people and processes. You end up creating magical possibilities.

I'm so grateful to have the opportunity to work with business owners such as Paul and to help husband and wife teams as well. It's an honor to make the journey with them as they change from being Fed up Freddy or Tired out Terry the technician, (extraordinarily good at what they do), to becoming extraordinary leaders, managers, and business owners who create and enjoy their ultimate business lifestyles.

My Why

After reading about Paul (and he is just one example—go to the "Success Stories" tab on www.ShirleyDalton.com for more examples), you might be wondering why I love doing what I do so much.

There are a number of reasons:

1. Growing up as an only child of taxi proprietors who worked long and hard for their money, I vowed I didn't

want other kids to grow up like me. There was money but no time. I can remember going on a family holiday—once. I remember sitting on my school bag shivering under a tiny umbrella on the veranda after school, dodging the rain, while waiting for mum to come home. That's not why you go into business for yourself. You go into business for the freedom you believe you'll have, and sadly most business owners find that they become slaves to their businesses. I don't want that for you. You don't want that for yourself or your family.

2. I love meeting and working with intelligent people. I am inspired by my clients. I am fascinated with people. I get to witness the cleverness of people as they create businesses from ideas. I get to learn so much about all sorts of businesses and industries and people.

3. I get to make a difference. In fact, my mission in life is to inspire, educate, and support you to be, do, have, and feel whatever it is that you want (as long as it's legal and moral). I do this by using my unique gifts, by talking with people, listening, and sharing my independent insights.

4. I love teaching and helping people to believe that it's possible to create their ultimate business lifestyle and I love seeing others dreams come true. Nothing makes me happier than to share the journey with others.

5. And of course, I can't help myself, systems are part of my DNA.

I know it's not only possible but it's probable for you to have a business and a life. I've helped hundreds of business owners to create their ultimate business lifestyle with my five-step system which I've refined over the past nine years.

Here are the five steps you need to take:

1. Make the decision and start working on yourself. Learn how to lead and manage yourself and others.

2. Identify and document your business workflow, from beginning to end for the customer experience. Flow chart who does what and when (and why) in your business.

3. Identify the roles you need to fulfill each task (roles, not people).

4. Create job descriptions. I like to call them *Key Performance Indicators* and *Key Behavior Indicators* so that everyone knows exactly what they have to do *and* to what standard to succeed in their roles.

5. Document your procedures. These are the *How* for every task identified in your workflow and your role descriptions.

The first step—making the decision and working on yourself—can be the hardest yet the most rewarding.

Don't waste any more time.

If you're a Fed up Freddy or Tired out Terry, get help.

Follow my triple P system—*People*, *Processes* and *Possibilities* to create your ultimate business lifestyle.

Go to www.BusinessFreedomFighters.com to download your free e-guide which will walk you through my ***5-Steps to Business Freedom*** in much more detail.

And as a bonus for purchasing this book and being the kind of business person who is open to professional development and to changing and improving the way you do things—the type of person who is open to the possibility and probability that you can create your ultimate business lifestyle—I invite you to apply for a complimentary consultation.

I can only offer this to a limited number of people, so if your application is accepted, I will work with you for up to ninety minutes to help you create your own business action plan, so you will know exactly what you need to do to improve your business, decrease stress, get your time back, and create your ultimate business lifestyle; in other words, create a plan for your freedom.

Just refer to the opportunity below to apply for your complimentary consultation. Use promotional code EBE-CC.

Shirley Dalton

Proven systems & strategies to create
your ultimate business lifestyle

Shirley's Special Offer:

Are you a *Fed Up Freddy* or *Tired Out Terry?*

Do you own a business but feel like the business owns you?
Are you feeling overwhelmed, stressed out, and OVER IT?
You could just walk away? TOO MUCH ON YOUR PLATE?

Good—you can change this! I can show you how
and it's easier than you think. You can create and live your
ultimate business lifestyle. You can own the business, make
money, and not have to work in it.

I've helped hundreds of other entrepreneurs
and business owners just like you.

If you'd like to apply for a one on one consultation with me
to develop your very own *Business Action Plan*, go to

http://shirleydalton.com/complimentary-consultation

and complete your application NOW.
Use promotional code EBE-CC
Places are limited.

64

About Shirley Dalton

Shirley Dalton is a sought-after speaker, best-selling author, and in-demand consultant for entrepreneurs and small business owners.

Formerly, Shirley was the Chief Operating Officer (COO) for an Australian international franchise organization. She was responsible for creating and streamlining internal systems and structures which enabled the company to list on the Australian Stock Exchange and grow from 250 franchises to over 600 worldwide.

Today, she specializes in developing people and processes. Using her *Triple P System for Business Success*, she works with you and your team to systemize and streamline your business so it works for you *and* your people.

Shirley's clients say they are free to live; no longer a martyr to their business. They can choose what they want to do with their time. For some it is travelling; for others it's playing sport; enjoying more family time; doubling their turnover without adding time or staff; saving themselves a day a month in time or selling their business to sail the world with their family.

Working with Shirley makes it possible to create and live your ultimate business lifestyle. To book Shirley for TV, visit http://ShirleyDalton.com/media and to book her for speaking engagements, visit http://ShirleyDalton.com/speaking.

To find out more about Shirley, visit http://www.ShirleyDalton.com

Chapter 6

Explode Your Productivity and Profits: The Missing Link to Workforce Wellness
by Donya Fahmy

"Insanity is doing the same thing over and over again and expecting different results."

-Albert Einstein

How many of you can relate to this now infamous quote that defines the meaning of the word *insanity*? It has been used so many times it's become almost ubiquitous, and I believe that's because you can take this statement and apply it to any area in your life or business and no matter what the circumstance, it still holds true.

I think it rings especially true when applied to the area of health and wellness—whether to your own personal health or the health of your workforce. So many times we blindly follow the conventional wisdom or whatever our doctors and health practitioners tell us is important. But people who suffer from chronic health challenges know that this approach doesn't always work so well.

How else can you explain the epidemic of chronic illness plaguing our society and ultimately the productivity and success of our businesses? According to WebMD.com, here in the United States alone, the estimated annual cost of allergies to businesses and the health care system is 7.9 BILLION dollars! Yes you read that right. That's just the impact of allergies.

A Milken Institute research study cited in a 2014 article in the *Harvard Business Review* concluded that common chronic diseases are responsible for 1.1 trillion dollars in lost productivity annually in the U.S. economy.

In fact a growing body of research, including a 2013 RAND Corporation study on "Workplace Wellness Programs," suggests that nurturing employee health and wellness has a significant impact on productivity, which has a direct bearing on company profitability.

If you don't currently offer some type of wellness initiative, you are not alone. But the increasing prevalence of chronic diseases in the working-age population will ultimately affect all businesses that don't take proactive measures to prevent it.

The Elephant in the Room

The Centers for Disease Control and Prevention (CDC) identified four behaviors—*inactivity, poor nutrition, tobacco use,* and *frequent alcohol consumption*—as primary causes of chronic disease in the United States. This is probably why typical wellness programs focus on "lifestyle management"— smoking cessation, weight loss, good nutrition, and fitness—all critically important elements of a wellness strategy. But there's an elephant in the room that nobody seems to be acknowledging that may be the missing piece to workforce wellness over the long haul.

It's something that most doctors won't tell their patients—simply because they don't know. It's not even on their radar. And that is the myriad of ways that our over-exposure to chemicals and toxins—in every aspect of our lives—is crippling our ability to overcome chronic health problems that eventually lead to chronic disease and skyrocket health care costs, while diminishing our productivity and profits.

An effective strategy for workplace wellness means reframing the mindset around health from one of "sickness" to one of "wellness."In this type of approach, you become partners in health with your employees rather than providers or facilitators of sick care.

As someone who suffered from chronic health problems for decades—both as an employee and as a business owner—and managed to overcome them, I can tell you that "bad health habits" are not the only thing you need to pay attention to.

From the time I started working in corporate America in my mid-twenties, I was dogged by a myriad of minor but somewhat chronic health problems from migraines and chronic fatigue to a range of recurring upper respiratory issues (chronic allergies, sinus infections, bronchitis, asthma), and ultimately eczema.

Looking back, I can say that I never thought of my health problems as "chronic" until I developed (from seemingly out of nowhere) a nasty case of recurring eczema that dogged me for seven years.

Bad Health Habits are Not the Only Problem

Most people think of eczema as an annoying skin condition—hardly something that would have a deleterious impact on one's productivity or absenteeism. But let me tell you, when it first came on, it was so severe I used to scratch myself in my sleep until I bled! When I was at work, I could barely make it through an hour without needing to run to the bathroom and have a secret scratch-fest to relieve all the itching.

Then there were those days where I would wake up, shower and get dressed for work, and within five minutes of putting on my pantyhose the unbearable itching would begin and I would have to get undressed and call in sick.

I doubt that my co-workers or my boss had any idea just how miserable I was, never mind how it was affecting my productivity. Nor could they possibly understand the stress and frustration I experienced as I went to a parade of dermatologists and doctors trying to find answers and solutions—to no avail.

None of the practitioners whose help I sought were able to identify the source of my problem. Not even close. To add insult to injury, they all prescribed essentially the same things—prescription strength antihistamines and cortisone—which obviously didn't work since the problem just kept coming back.

Lather, rinse, repeat. Remember the quote about the definition of Insanity?

I finally just hit a wall and decided to take matters into my own hands. I've always been the type of person who, when faced with a challenge or problems, becomes determined to find a better solution. At the time, I had already been dabbling in aromatherapy just as a hobby and had acquired a small collection of essential oils and a variety of books on the subject.

After some research and experimentation, I made my own blend that I applied topically and guess what? Within a day or two my itching and inflammation were completely under control. WOW! This little blend was about as effective as the cortisone shots I had been taking, without the threat of all the nasty side effects.

That AHA moment was the impetus for creating Dropwise Essentials—my line of aromatherapy and natural personal care products. I became obsessed with herbs, flowers, and plants as "medicine" and started my research and inquiry into how to use these ingredients to create everyday products that would help other people achieve health and wellness, using safer, natural alternatives.

Not only did this simple natural solution help me cope with my challenging symptoms in a safe, non-habit forming way, it actually helped me overcome the condition. The next time I had an outbreak of eczema, I simply applied my blend topically and supplemented it with an herbal tincture for liver support. When that episode cleared up, I was *totally free of eczema for nearly ten years!*

But just when I thought I finally had this thing licked, I had a nasty recurrence of skin trouble—really serious hives that lasted for four months. Nothing in my plant arsenal seemed to work so that's when I sought the help of a homeopath. We worked together for about three years and were able to resolve all of my skin issues as well as some other lingering health problems. But more importantly, through this work, I learned a critical piece of information: medication can sometimes thwart the body's efforts to heal itself, which can lead to developing one or more seemingly unrelated conditions.

That's what happened with my eczema. My body was trying to move my upper respiratory problem (asthma) away from my lungs (a vital organ) to a less vital organ (my skin). Research shows a definite link between asthma and eczema, and you see this happening a lot in small children—especially infants. They *are* related.

What Worked for Me Can Work for You

Embracing a holistic, toxin-free lifestyle has been my salvation. That is why I'm on a mission to help others find kinder, gentler, and more sustainable ways to address their health issues and reclaim their wellness —both in the workplace and at home. I credit my lasting success to three primary decisions:

1. Getting off medications and finding safer plant-based alternatives

2. Not relying strictly on what doctors told me to do—especially when it didn't work—and finding alternative practitioners for support in taking a different approach

3. Relentlessly and systematically reducing my exposure to chemicals and toxins in all areas of my life—food, personal care products, and home and environmental health

How do I know what works? Over the past twenty-five years, I can count on one hand the number of times I've been to a physician's office—and that would include the last two visits I made to a doctor regarding my eczema. As of this writing, my last MD visit was ten years ago.

During that same time I have not taken *any* prescription medications, and with the exception of some recent dental procedures, I've not taken any antibiotics either.

I share my story and these results not to impress, but to illustrate two important points:

1. When it comes to one's productivity and ability to focus, minor chronic health problems can be just as consuming and distracting as major ones.

2. Our health is NOT a one-size-fits-all prescription and what we don't see CAN hurt us.

We live in an increasingly complex and toxic world that's creating endless health challenges that require a more intelligent and focused approach than the one-size-fits-all, cookie-cutter approach we typically get from traditional medicine, health care systems, and corporate wellness initiatives.

Eliminating the root cause of any problem is the fastest and most effective way of solving it. Your health is no exception. But with so many possible sources or causes, the challenge of identifying them can seem daunting. One can feel like they're in a maze with no way out.

If we look at this type of situation as a labyrinth rather than a dead-end, then we know there is a way out, it just may take some time and some innovative thinking to find it.

Some of it is just basic common sense and surprisingly simple, yet no one is really out there teaching it, and most people are often on their own when it comes to deciphering the avalanche of confusing and sometimes conflicting health information that's available to them.

It's the Immune System, Silly!

The simple truth is that in most cases, strengthening your immune system and keeping it strong is your best strategy for addressing and resolving health issues—especially chronic health challenges. But you can't adequately strengthen your immune system by adding boosters and support if you don't also eliminate the various sources of exposure to toxins and allergens that weaken us and secretly rob us of our health and vitality. It's a balancing act for sure.

If I had to sum up the missing piece in our healthcare puzzle it's this: the hidden health mines in our food, personal care, and household products are the real silent killers.

Routine exposure to countless seemingly harmless chemicals in our everyday products add up to an ongoing assault on our immune systems, and can often be the very things that trigger allergies or other forms of upper respiratory inflammation as well as skin disorders. Add to that the industrialization of our agriculture and you have a food supply that is not only deficient in nutrients, but also polluted with a variety of toxins from heavy metals and pesticides to Genetically Modified Organisms (GMOs). This is wreaking havoc with our digestive systems—the seat of our health.

Any truly successful wellness initiative or strategy (whether new or established) needs to take these factors into account.

Here's my ten-point prescription for wellness success in the workplace:

1. Educate your employees on the different (hidden and not so hidden) ways their health is being compromised on a regular basis.

2. Make it less clinical and more lifestyle oriented by bringing awareness to what I call the *3 Pillars of Whole Health*: what they put in their mouth, rub on their skin, and allow or introduce into their environments (i.e. what they breathe in).

3. Do no harm. Make sure your office environments are free of hidden toxins, and if you provide food and drink, offer only healthy, additive-free, low-sugar and sugar-free options

4. Support them in learning to become smart, healthy shoppers by just saying "*No*" to products made with toxic or potentially harmful ingredients, and "*Yes*" to healthier alternatives.

5. Expand the range of diagnostic tools and assessments available to help them better pinpoint their underlying issues.

6. Encourage them to explore alternative approaches instead of always following the path of least resistance (i.e. seeking medical treatment for every ailment).

7. Focus on offering them natural holistic solutions to better manage their stress and stressors—both in the workplace and at home.

8. Tap into their personal motivations and reward them for achieving critical milestones.

9. Tie all wellness activities back to a broader company strategy and mission.

10. Harness the power of shared accountability to sustain engagement and make it fun!

Donya Fahmy
Natural Holistic Solutions to Finally Get Your Life Back

Donya's Special Offer:

If you want to know the best ways to become a partner in wellness with your workforce, you can start by reading a copy of Donya's complimentary guide,

Heal Yourself Naturally: 3 Steps to Life Changing Results

Use these three steps as a framework to help you identify where you can truly support your employees in overcoming chronic health issues and set them up for success in creating productive lives of vibrant health and wellness.

Get your copy at:
http://www.YourHiddenHealthMines.com

Then schedule a FREE no-obligation one-on-one consultation with Donya to identify what your next best move is for creating or re-focusing your workplace wellness strategies and offerings to maximize productivity so you can explode your profit.

About Donya Fahmy

Donya Fahmy is America's leading advocate for plant-based healing and your Natural Health and Wellness Mentor. She is the CEO, Founder, and Formulator for Dropwise Essentials—a green health and wellness company specializing in aromatherapy and natural solutions for personal care.

After suffering from chronic allergies, asthma, and eczema, for almost two decades, Donya was able to finally heal herself using natural and plant-based solutions to successfully accomplish what doctors and traditional medicine couldn't. She was inspired to create the Dropwise product line after making an aromatherapy solution for her eczema that worked almost as effectively as the numerous steroid medications she had been taking.

Donya has been formulating aromatherapy and organic personal care products for more than fourteen years and empowers women to take control of their health and wellness. Using her extensive knowledge and experience, she's pioneered a simple five-step system called the Allergy Clean Sweep that anyone can use to naturally heal or prevent chronic health problems. With it, she mentors and supports individuals, families, and companies in identifying and eliminating the sources of their persistent health challenges, and introduces them to natural and holistic solutions that help them heal so they can reclaim their wellness and finally get their lives back.

To find out more about Donya, visit http://www.DonyaFahmy.com

Chapter 7

Are You Letting Negative Karma Get in the Way of Your Success?
by Paramahansa Jagadish

"Karma moves in two directions. If we act virtuously, the seed we plant will result in happiness. If we act non-virtuously, suffering results."

−Sakyong Mipham

What goes around, comes around.
What you give, you get.
Every action has an equal and opposite reaction.
What you sow, you reap.

These are some of the expressions that express the *Law of Karma*, otherwise known as the *Law of Cause and Effect*. The movie *Pay It Forward* was a wonderful way to introduce us to the benefits—both personal and social—of giving and therefore helping others, but to do it in ways that truly serve the other, the one you are gifting to. These types

79

of actions create good karma. Good karma brings good things into our lives.

When we smile at someone or do a small favor showing respect, consideration, and warmth, the recipient feels good and is likely to do the same to someone else within minutes. These small acts of kindness become contagious . . . and when they do, what a wonderful world it is.

The Sanskrit word karma means "action." Karmas are actions. The implication and shades of meaning attached to this word relates to the *Law of Karma*, which implies: do good to others and others will do good to you; make trouble to others and trouble will be presented to you; cause others to suffer and indeed you will suffer in the future. This Causal Law relates to the soul. The soul is what lives on after death. So karma follows us to our future lives, ready to manifest at any place, any time, any life. This is why it is difficult at times to see this law in action and therefore understand its power directly.

Many times we receive the results of our past life karma— positive or negative—in this life, and cannot make sense of it. When we see negative karma play out in people who are kind and virtuous, it hurts us and we become angry towards God or life itself. What we want to remember here is that karma is here for us to learn virtue and compassion. It is not set-up as outright punishment, but as chances to learn life lessons and grown as a human being. When we work with our karma, we gain the lessons and mature as human beings. This is good!

Now I want to talk with you about the importance of creating good karma in relation to success in business and in life!

We create good karma by doing good deeds and giving to worthy causes, by diminishing lack and suffering for others, saving lives, and making others happy. The secret is to perform the above without any selfish motivation and without any need or desire whatsoever for reward. It is done humbly out of loving service. We also do this without any desire for acknowledgement or praise. We can smile if it comes!

Along with creating good karma we want to make sure we reduce acting and speaking in ways that produce bad karma. We want to think a bit before we react toward others or situations in life.

Here is a simply story for us to understand how easy it is to create bad karma for ourselves as well as for others. A person comes home from a long troubled day at work. The family dog welcomes this person with licks and a waging tail. The person—tired and fed-up—kicks the dog away and grumbles. This person transferred the frustration of the day at work onto the family dog. The dog is innocent and yet got undeserved treatment. The dog suffered for the treatment meant for someone else. Here in this action bad karma was created for the person we are discussing. (Extend this idea to many of our relationship interactions and the rest of this chapter will be very helpful for you).

This is why it is important to live a life of virtue. It is very worthwhile to spend time thinking about the different virtues in order to imbibe them. Without virtues such as honesty, etc. we have no integrity. If we do not keep our word in business interactions we will get less and less business; the same in intimate relationships, etc.

We all have three areas of awareness, or minds if you will: the conscious, the sub-conscious, and the unconscious. Many of us are hardly aware of all the content in our conscious mind, let alone the other two. But it is the content in all three of them that affect us, affect others, and affect our

81

circumstances in life. In a way, each one of us is the Pig Pen character from the *Charlie Brown* cartoons . . . we carry all of our varied content with us, swirling around us and affecting all we come in contact with. It is the conscious and sub-conscious mind content that shows people who and what we are on a human level, and is intuited by others to the degree that they are able to perceive it. All of us have had some experience in our lives of meeting someone we liked a lot right away, or another whom we did not want to meet or be around.

At times there are extreme cases of what I am conveying to you, such as when someone walks into a room and people feel fear or danger in some way that they cannot quite understand (other than that particular person has "bad vibes" and I don't want to be around them). Or, somewhere else someone walks into a room and we feel uplifted and are attracted to this person and want to meet them. They have an infectious smile, etc.

When we understand what this is, we can do certain things that give an immediate "good vibes" to all those who see us and come into our sphere. It has to do with a depth and prevalence of cleanliness, honesty, willingness to help others, and happiness. When our negative habits, attitudes, biases, and conditioning are cleansed out of our conscious, sub-conscious, and as much as possible out of our unconscious, the Light of the Self shines out for all to feel, sense and experience. Thus, you have attained the natural projection of "Good Vibes" wherever you go, to whomever you meet. This is true and genuine success. Inner success like this leads quickly to outer success.

Thoughts, feelings, and emotions have and carry energy; they all have energetic content. Depending on the nature of our thoughts, feelings, and emotions, we carry a vibe around with us. Happy, sad, confused, fearful, angry, resentful, lazy, greedy, dishonest, disappointed, arrogant, low self-esteem, deceptive, and delusional are some examples. We might try to cover over these energies with enthusiasm through affirmations and an upbeat attitude—which can be helpful— but it will lack the integrity we want in our lives and the positive impact it can have on others. Therefore, when we understand how all this works in our circumstances in life, and in the situations that arise—especially the ones that repeat themselves—we can begin to learn its importance and become interested in how to remedy it.

One way to look at this is that we have different aspects to ourselves other than "me the body," "me the mind," or "me the personality." We can look at it inclusively as our soul. The soul is composed of a record of all our past experience and actions. In this world our soul comes into a body complex where it again learns about itself and life on this planet. I call this complex the *Psycho-physical Field of Body/Mind/Soul*. We can say that not only do we have a physical body—this physical form—but we also have a mental aspect to us that we can call the mental body or form, and the emotional body and others that many of us have not heard of.

The astral body is a vehicle we have and use to travel at nighttime when our physical body is sleeping. Anyone remember having vivid dreams, ones that seem so realistic? Some of these are direct experiences you have while traveling in your astral body.

The idea here is a proactive one of clearing the negative karmic content from our meta-physical constituents through healing treatments and spiritual practices!

Besides these bodies, we have meta-physical instruments and other interfaces between our purely physical existence and the subtle sides of our meta-physical nature. Many have heard about the Chakras or spinning wheel-like energy centers that interface to our physical body through specific organs called glands. These major energy centers also hold specific emotions and attitudes, colors, sound, and frequencies. When they are dull or lethargic, they create imbalance of energy frequencies, which make the color of them darker or "off," which then increases our feeling out of balance, out of tune, and otherwise unhappy and negative.

We also have the Meridian Lines that can have the same imbalances from life's stresses, such as working too fast, or they can become slow and sluggish, or actually blocked, which then manifests in dis-ease of some kind or another.

When the above body/mind/soul complexes are cleansed, one feels so good . . . good about ourselves, good about others and good about the world! It's like taking a shower after days of not being able to—the feeling of being wonderfully refreshed, or like drinking pure clean water after twenty-four hours of not having any liquids (have you ever had this experience?).

The above can also be cleansed out by yogic practices including their physical exercises that have become so popular, but most importantly the practice of virtue, prayer, and meditation. Similar kinds of full-spectrum spiritual practices can be performed in Buddhism, Hinduism, Taoism, Hawaiian, and other Indigenous Traditions that have this cleansing effect.

A good energy healer can address the above and help cleanse this level of interference in our lives (please be sure to hire someone who is genuine and has true compassion and integrity). Otherwise, there are also the newer spiritual traditions of pure light coming out of Japan, like Jorei.

Receiving treatments from these centers is very nice and with consistency are very effective to uplift us in profound ways.

Why the Work I Do is So Important

Everyone would like to be more successful and prosperous, but most don't realize the simple truths regarding the content of their unconscious attitudes and patterns that are keeping them from reaching their full potential. Just like any physical malady, you cannot fix the problem without knowing its source. Karma Clearing goes to the causal source of the problems, issues, and obstacles we face in life. The private work I perform in the causal level of Karma Clearing works to improve lives that usually takes years of regular sessions with others. Miracles from the efficacy of the private sessions, and all the work I do, is known by the many people who work with me, many of them master healers themselves, and people of the medical industry.

Have you ever wanted to be free from your personal suffering . . . from having bad days, and the stress and frustrations that go along with them . . . to live a life of joy and divine accomplishment?

I help sincere individuals clear away lifetimes of negative karmic blockages and ancestral obstacles that keep them from experiencing the profound self-empowerment, joy, and success of a truly empowered life.

Transform your life from a life of negative patterns and limitations that cause suffering in your life and hinder your forward growth. By getting to the deepest cause of these problems and issues in your life, and removing them, the results are miraculous!

Through the clearing and eradication of lifetimes of suffering and bondage on the karmic causal level, people open up spontaneously to more and more of their inner potential, creating a wave of self-empowerment that brings greater and greater success. Every session I do with others—with you—bestows deeper and deeper levels of self-empowerment, freedom, happiness, and profound well-being.

Sacred Energy Devices—
Life-Saving Miracles that Everyone Can Use!

The good news is that there is a way to get the above cleansing in the privacy of your own home with the extraordinary Sacred Energy Devices Divinity has made available to the public.

Why you want to purchase and use Sacred Energy Devices: There are hundreds of major and minor miracles attributed to these devices used by people from all walks of life from around the globe. Many spiritually attained teachers and master healers have been astounded by the power, purity, and inconceivable energy of these sacred devices, let alone amazed at the work they do. It is impossible to imagine that a normal object such as a card, light bulb, or sticker can have the power to cleanse negative energy from whatever they engage. This is exactly the case with these Sacred Energy Devices. Paramahansa Jagadish has the ability to hold the purist Divine Energy within his body that transforms, empowers, and actually configures these objects to do what they do.

The Sacred Energy Devices

The Sacred Energy Devices are configured to cleanse and purify objects, people, places, things, and circumstances, of

86

negative energy content. Touch them to the objects (or their representations—photographs, writings, etc) and the devices will cleanse them. Tune in while using them and you will happily become aware of their energetic capacities.

The Sacred Energy Card/Energy Sticker

The Sacred Energy Card will purify anything it is touched to. It will purify objects of any negative thoughts, feelings, emotions, or vibrations that it holds. Touch it to your plate of food before you eat; it will purify the food from any negativity from the people and processes it has gone through. Clients who carry it in their wallet on trips do not experience negative effects from jet-lag. If you have trouble sleeping, put it under your pillow before bed. There are unlimited uses the card can address; the only limit is your imagination! Experiment with it and let me know what effects you have noticed! The stickers work in the same way, becoming activated when they are adhered to something. Adhere them to your TVs(s), computer(s), phone(s), chairs, beds, light switches, credit cards, checkbooks, and date/activity books and see the results!

The Sacred Energy Light Bulb

Like the other Sacred Energy Devices, the Blue Bulb has the capacity to cleanse and purify negative energy from any object it shines on. Shinning in a room, it will purify the atmosphere, objects, people, and other things in the room. One great use is to fill-up any glass jar(s) with drinking water and place it (them) under the blue light for two full hours. This will purify and energize the water so much that the water will purify your body! Drink this water all the time, as it works as a powerful preventative to future health issues. Plants (and animals) love this water! Rinse your fruit and vegetables with it! Put some in the bath, and in the washing machine while washing clothes. Use your imagination!

What cannot be addressed with the Sacred Energy Devices above—as wonderful and powerful as they are—is the heaviest of negative karma that we carry in the unconscious mind. This is the content from all our past lives. This is where the many blocks and obstacles to a successful life are held, and try as we may to have success in our lives for ourselves and family, the causal negative content continues to cause lack and suffering.

To not add to this content we need to be honest, virtuous people with full integrity. To clear this content we need to do good deeds—lots and lots of good deeds—hours of deep meditation each day, and a few other advanced things— secrets from ancient India. Also, you can hire the services of someone who can access and clear this deepest level of negative karma. To advance into a super-human-being, to realize our full potential in a quick and realistic way, I sincerely suggest both . . . doing the work we can do ourselves and also getting help from someone qualified.

Guide to Things You Can Do Yourself

Clearing deep levels of negative karma opens up and empowers us to greater and greater health, wellbeing, love, happiness, and success. Therefore I want to now give an outline of things you can do for yourselves on the path to perpetual "Good Vibes."

The How to Part—*Exercises*

Exercise one:

Practice a sincere and heartfelt gratitude all throughout your day, for the love, happiness, and health that you do have. This will make everything seem brighter for yourself and others.

Exercise two:

Write down a list of the people you have borrowed from and never re-paid. People you have stolen from and never gave back, people you have harmed and never made amends, people you have lied to for self-gain and never made right.

Exercise three:

Make amends to the above people in whatever way you can! Pay them back with interest and a heart-felt apology, asking them for forgiveness. Figure out ways to heal the wounds that create mistrust and bad feelings.

Exercise four:

Take some time each day to sit silently and focus on the breath. This builds self-awareness and concentration. Try counting the in-breath and the out-breath as one cycle and count to twenty one cycles. If you lose track of the count, start at one again (when you notice the thoughts that take your conscious awareness away from the breath, recognize it and gently bring your awareness back to the cycle of the breath starting the count at one again).

Experiment with the suggested practices below and see if they open your heart and mind and increase your successes in life (of course we want to do these activities in an unconditional, selfless way):

1. Smile to those you love and others you encounter each day (as you feel it is appropriate).

2. Clean the house and yard regularly.

3. Purchase protein bars and stash away some clean dollar bills. Have them available in your car or knapsack to give to homeless people of your choice who you meet in the course of your day. If for any reason you do not see such people, then make a point to go to the areas where they are and give to them there. (It helps to do this in sincerity, with the attitude that they would be doing this for you if the circumstances were opposite).

4. Pray and/ or meditate each day as a gift to yourself, to others, and to world peace!

5. Do good deeds for others, especially for those you love, the elderly, the disadvantaged, and for children, including chores around their houses and yards.

For more advanced work and insight into the human condition, study and reflect upon the ego defense mechanisms and work on reducing them in your day-to-day interactions with others.

Jagadish's Special Offer:

Because you are reading this guide and have become a part of Jagadish's community, we invite you to a *Free Discovery Call* so we can explore the best options for your journey.

Would you like to experience continued spiritual growth? Would like to be released from negative patterns that are holding you back?

If you're not truly happy, at peace, fulfilled, or haven't realized unconditional love, then your true nature is obscured by karmic blockages.

Get started right now. Go to
http://www.YourSacredSoul.com

Then email Events@EvolvethePlanet.com or call toll free 877-838-1133 to book your call. We'll see you on the inside.

Paramahansa Jagadish

"Your Personal Guide to Divine Connection and Limitless Possibilities"

About Paramahansa Jagadish

Grand Master Healer and Liberated Spiritual Master Paramahansa Jagadish's level of spiritual attainment allows the Divine to be directly expressed through him, leading you to your own ultimate transformation! His Western education includes a graduate degree in Transpersonal Psychology, but what truly sets him apart from a million other practitioners is that he is a Liberated Spiritual "Grand Master" Healer and Lineage holder.

Jagadish's journey began at age four and led him to the very heart of India, where he spent twelve years in intensive spiritual study, living with Holy "God-Realized" Rishis. Through deep devotion and practice, Jagadish earned the title of "Paramahansa" while attaining true and genuine liberation (Self-Realization), the first level of God-Realization, as well as the profound abilities of taking on and burning-up the deepest levels of Karma in others. His healing work awakens the heart to experience Divine Grace . . .the source of all transformation.

Jagadish has helped thousands, including celebrities, spiritual teachers, military personnel, animals, and houses, projects, and businesses. The more one works with Jagadish, the more one's consciousness evolves towards the experience of profound illumination and a deeper connection to God. You too can take advantage of the rare opportunity to work with him while he is still available to the public.

**To find out more about Jagadish, visit
http://www.EvolveThePlanet.com**

92

Chapter 8

Empowering and Engaging Your Groups through Travel
by Suzi Nelsen

Did you ever have an idea and think it was just crazy enough to work? If so, you are not alone.

About a year ago, I had an epiphany. After having volunteered for over fourteen years at Porter's Hospice in Denver, I came to realize that everyone on the outside of hospice always wants to know: *"What do you do for a living?"* and *"How much money do you make?"*

Within hospice the questions and the answers are entirely different. At the end of life, the most important answers a person can give you about their lives are: who they love, where they have been, and what they regret. This extreme contrast in mentalities and values was the catalyst for a defining moment for me. As a result, I made a life-changing decision to become a person who was determined to make businesses and companies more profitable, by creating opportunities to remove regrets in people's lives.

Defining the Problem

"In the last twenty years, the amount of time Americans have spent at their jobs has risen steadily."

-Juliet B. Schor

In a random survey, conducted in 2008 by the Work Foundation, of five hundred individuals, seventy-five percent of full-time workers admitted their productivity and satisfaction was affected by a wish to spend more time with their families. Not surprisingly, the same study revealed individuals working overtime as only half as likely as those working part-time to be satisfied with their work. Additionally, individuals working forty or more hours per week were only half as likely as part-time workers to claim they were happy with their work/life balance.

A 2014 study on flexible workplace policies conducted by Harris Interactive, revealed married or partnered workers, who consider themselves primarily responsible for the household's income, continuously struggle to log adequate family time. Additionally, over seventy percent of workers polled indicated they were not given enough time to spend with their families.

These findings show professionals today are seeing a lot less of their families and a lot more of their cubicles and offices. In her book, *The Overworked American*, author Juliet B. Schor presented an alarming but very relevant fact: workers today are now on the job more than one month longer per year than employed individuals were forty-five years ago.

Full-time employees spend forty plus hours at work each week, and when it comes time for them to take a vacation, a lot of them end up spending this time away from their families, because the travel reward incentive offered by employers does not include benefits for the rest of the family. In addition, dual income families are forced to make financial sacrifices when one of them is required to take unpaid time away from work to travel with his or her partner on their corporate-sponsored incentive vacation.

The Benefits of Balancing Happiness and Success

"If everyone is happy moving forward together,
then success takes care of itself."

-Henry Ford

A recent Gallup report concluded that a mere thirteen percent of employees globally are actively engaged in their work. Furthermore, in a study commissioned by Right Management, University of Wisconsin's research concluded that bolstering the engagement of employees leads to higher financial performance, higher customer satisfaction, and higher employee retention. The Right Management 2008-2009 global benchmarking study supported these findings. Finally, in another study, other researchers found that sixty-seven percent of workers disclosed that they felt more productive after returning from vacation (Ranstad study, "Out of Office, But not Away from Work", 2014).

Incorporating a travel incentive program that allows employees to have the opportunity to include entire families on incentive travel vacations through "family reward programs" will not only act as a means for motivation at work, but also will strengthen professional relationships and increase profitability across the board. Each and every one of us want to maintain a sense of harmony throughout our lifetime, whether you are a stay-at-home mom or dad, a working mother or father, a CEO, a student, or simply anyone traveling this road of life.

Working together and traveling together will support growth and value to the company. As family and friends work and travel together, they also cooperate together. This leads to the dynamics of synergy and can create solutions to problems that might otherwise not have been solved. Another benefit of a cooperative team culture is that happy employees will recruit friends and relatives to work at a company that they enjoy working for, thereby reducing recruiting costs. Great companies get acknowledged by becoming a local "Great Place to Work." This in turn raises the public perception of the company, saving advertising and marketing costs.

Numerous studies have concluded that happy employees are healthy employees. Healthy employees take fewer sick days. As health care deductibles continue to rise, this will lead to a push to seek ways to reduce employee absenteeism. Offering family vacation incentives provides compelling reasons for new hires and seasoned employees to obtain value-added benefits to their existing employment benefits while reducing absentee costs to employers.

This ability to include families on corporate-sponsored vacations will benefit employees and corporations alike. Employees will be able to develop a heightened bond amongst their co-workers and families. Corporations on the other hand will accrue employees who feel a balance between their personal and professional life, thus expanding their engagement in the workplace.

96

As stated earlier, it is true that at the end of our lives we will also want to share with someone about the people we have loved, the places we have been to, and our regrets. Corporations are now in a unique position to be an example to peers and their communities by taking a hard look at their current incentive travel programs and including the families of their employees. This will provide the needed framework to build lasting memories and remove regrets from the lives of others.

Increasing Productivity Through Expanded Travel Incentives

*"Life is not measured by the breaths you take,
but by the moments that take your breath away"*

-Hilary Cooper

Through incentive travel, Countries and Crossroads can help to increase lucrative and productive connections with work peers for its clients. Additionally, expanding the scope of travel incentive benefits to include families will boost and strengthen family relationships, thereby increasing employee work engagement and reducing employee absenteeism.

Our company addresses three main categories for prosperous business incentive travel, which include custom plans, increasing community, and corporate culture in order to achieve and exceed the wants, needs, and goals of each client. Our corporate group department actively works to consolidate families into incentive travel packages,

97

which companies and corporations can offer their employees. We help corporations easily incentivize top producers so they can retain their best employees—keeping them engaged while increasing the productivity for the company.

Countries and Crossroads has planned trips for groups of a few to groups of 22,000. For example, we had the honor to serve Gary Barnes, CEO of GaryBarnesInternational.com, who approached us to facilitate travel for over 12,000 people from all over the world for a specialized custom event.

"Countries and Crossroads were on site and overseeing our event which was a huge undertaking, bringing people in from all over the world . . . helping everyone with airline tickets, accommodations, vehicles, tours, community service, and transportation to name a few. Suzi and her staff were always available and made this size event seem effortless, especially transporting 12,000 people every day for one week from Denver to Red Rocks Stadium. Suzi took a personal interest in everyone that was coming at her from every direction and her calm demeanor prevailed over the event. I highly recommend Countries and Crossroads for your group travel needs." -Gary Barnes

Smart companies pride themselves on creating a corporate family environment and it is our intention to help as many corporations understand the value of including families into their incentive travel programs as possible. Countries and Crossroads offers a profitable way for corporations to reward productivity and reinforce corporate values and bonding, by including family in incentive reward travel.

Instead of success *or* family, we can help our clients provide success *with* family. Our measure of fulfillment entails combining these values. Providing for the families within your business will enrich both your company and your community. By implementing a one-of-a-kind proven strategy to touch both areas of influence, Countries and Crossroads can help you to:

- Increase the profitability of your company

- Increase employee productivity and job satisfaction

- Increase employee family time and bonding, which includes company families

- Increase employee engagement and bonding among peers both within your company as well as within the family of associated companies.

Everyone wants to be part of a winning team, and incentive family travel provides colleagues and their families with the opportunity for bonding. We have spent a countless amount of time researching various options in order to develop a successful program that costs your corporation virtually nothing and can help your business increase its bottom line.

Countries and Crossroads is not just a travel company; our motto is *"The best advocate for your company is your happiest employee."* We specialize in corporate group travel, helping families increase lifetime memories while fulfilling employer's desires to increase productivity and profitability. This is taking place in an overreaching drive to reduce lifetime regrets and replace them with lasting memories spent with loved ones instead.

Increasing Loyalty Through Expanded Travel Incentives

"A five percent increase in customer retention can increase lifetime profits from that client by seventy-five percent."

-Frederick Reichheld, author of *The Loyalty Effect.*

While our groups are focused on incentive travel, we also assist businesses and corporations that have members rather than employees, such as publishers, authors, speakers, networking groups, and more. The list is limitless. These groups are brought together for educational purposes and to create organized and high-value experiences.

In most cases these experiences revolve around annual events and quarterly retreats.

Having thirty years of experience as a single mom raising three amazing sons has forged in me faith and an ability to generate income and value, while creating meaning in my own life. I have been able to—despite all the difficulties associated with being a businesswoman and a single mother—produce lifetime memories for my family while traveling the world. I feel strongly about offering the same for my clients.

Richard Branson of Virgin Records and Forbes top ten billionaires acknowledged, *"Time is the new currency."* One of the biggest regrets of many is they did not take the time they had to create memories with the ones they love.

100

You don't have to be a rocket scientist to know that value and success stems from long-term habits and values. In order to be profitable in our personal and professional life, we need to make money while creating meaning. Countries and Crossroads also provides the *Happy at Home, Successful at Work Webinar*™ to help corporations and their associated families achieve their goals.

You will benefit from working with Countries and Crossroads through our commitment to creating timeless memories for you and your loved ones, while promoting the management of workplace relationships.

We understand that life can get busy and moments can be lost too quickly, which is why we pride ourselves on saving you time and frustration in the incentive travel planning process. We understand the amount of buying power that goes into organizing your travel plans, and the negotiation skills and the many major details that to go into creating your lifetime memory trip.

Countries and Crossroads has the ability to collaborate directly with knowledgeable professionals in the travel industry. In addition, our professionals are committed to putting forth the necessary effort to obtain buying power, negotiation skills, and attention to the tiniest of details, all of which play a significant role in creating that lifetime memory trip you, your company employees, and families will cherish forever.

Countries and Crossroads would be honored to assist your company or your organization in creating lifetime memories for your associates and their families.

What are you waiting for? Contact us to see how this reward program works and how it will benefit your company. Life begins now, in this moment. Gaining meaning in life requires reflection, great values, great memories, and great places celebrated, shared, and experienced with loved ones.

Are you living this life and allowing your employees to live it, too? Do you believe it cannot be done profitably? Let Countries and Crossroads show you how. Now.

Suzi's Special Offer:

Give yourself the gift of creating lifetime memories!

If you want to learn how to travel
the world for free while cruising,

Get Your Free Consultation at:

www.IncentiveTravelRewards.com

About Suzi Nelsen

Suzi Nelsen is a corporate group and incentive travel expert and is the founder of Countries and Crossroads.

With thirty plus years of experience in world travel, and as a successful entrepreneur, Suzi understands that negotiating the intricate details of group travel can be challenging, and she is dedicated to providing world-class service at all levels.

Suzi is an international speaker and speaks on negotiation and relationship skills.

Suzi started her career as a travel agent at the age of twenty-two, and founded her first agency by the time she was twenty-five. She grew her business to include offices in Denver, New York, London, and San Diego.

She received the Dale Carnegie's Leadership Certification of achievement, the Harvard University Leadership Achievement Certification, and has been recognized by *Who's Who of Executive Professionals and Entrepreneurs*.

Suzi has traveled the world extensively with her children and she is very passionate about helping people create memories that last a lifetime. She helps you develop a corporate culture that supports incentives and family travel to create an environment that results in maximizing retention, engagement, and productivity.

**To find out more about Suzi, visit
http://www.CountriesAndCrossroads.com**

Chapter 9

Your Energized Self:
Feeding Your Mind, Body, and Spirit
by Andrena Taylor

Have you ever noticed how a meal makes you feel? Have you felt heavy or sluggish, experienced bloating, headaches, cravings, or foggy thinking? Or perhaps you almost fall asleep at your desk after lunch.

Although I have always been interested in eating wholesome nutritious foods, I have not always followed what my heart knew to be best for my body. Life and busy schedules took over and I fell into the fast food trap. Fifty percent of the time I paid attention to what I was putting into my body, and the other fifty percent—well, not the ideal diet.

Our bodies are very resilient and patient, but eventually symptoms and issues appear. That is what happened to me. I started experiencing major digestive problems which would often keep me up at night. I didn't immediately pay attention and the digestive issues became more and more intense. This led me to seek out a naturopathic doctor to help me sort out what was bothering me. After undergoing testing, I was surprised to find that foods I have always loved to eat, were now causing me problems. For me these were dairy, eggs, mushrooms, and wheat. After eliminating these foods, my digestive issued started to alleviate. This led me to read more and more information on organic foods, gluten free cooking and healthy eating, and eventually led me to change careers and become a holistic nutritionist.

What I have learned is that everyone is biochemically unique and food can change your mood. How you feed your body will affect your mood and how you feel about your body affects your food choices. You will have more energy if you choose good-mood foods rather than bad-mood foods that provide a temporary lift followed by a crash. When you take care of your body, you will have a healthy and joyous place to live for years.

Do you want to feel energized and have an enthusiasm for living? The strategies below will help you on your journey to wellness—feeding your mind, body, and spirit.

Mindful Eating—Practice Gratitude

Mindful eating means taking the time to be grateful for the food set before you by appreciating the flavors, textures, and colors. This allows you to slow down from your busy schedule to take time to enjoy your meals. Today, too many people eat at their desk while working, or in the car while rushing somewhere; or they eat on a couch while watching television. If you don't take the time to relax while you are eating, your digestion becomes impaired, as eating while stressed slows down digestion and causes discomfort, and results in poor assimilation of vitamins and minerals. Slowing down the process of eating prevents overeating, and allows you to truly enjoy the food before you. Mindful eating also includes taking the time to choose nutrient dense whole foods, and avoid pre-packaged foods which are full of additives and preservatives. Choosing foods that are close to their natural state honors your body and your health. Taking the time to prepare your meals and sharing them with your family and friends also honors your spirit—as meals should be eaten with your loved ones, and allows you to reconnect with them in a relaxed way.

Give Your Body What it Needs

Drink Water

Are you drinking enough pure water? Our bodies are comprised of sixty percent water; our brains are made up of eighty-five percent water. Water is the primary component of all the bodily fluids—blood, lymph, digestive juices, urine, tears, and sweat, and is involved in almost every bodily function. Water also is important for healing. Well hydrated bodies perform at their peak and give you abundant energy.

Many clients come to me complaining of dry skin, or constipation, or experiencing heartburn. These are all signs that they are not drinking enough water. The average person should consume a minimum of eight cups of water a day, in addition to the water that is released from the fruit and vegetables that are consumed. Coffee, tea, and other beverages do not add to the water requirement, and in some cases—such as coffee, which is a diuretic—upsets our water balance. If you are thirsty, this is a sign that you are already dehydrated. Dry skin is another marker, as our skin is our largest organ and can be an indicator of inadequate water consumption. A good way to ensure that you drink enough water is to consume a cup of water for every hour you are awake. Keep a water bottle by your desk to remind yourself to drink your water. Ensure that the water you drink is pure.

Avoid drinking tap water; invest in a water filter. Purchasing pre-bottled water is an unnecessary expense if you have a good quality system at home. Plastic store bought water has the risk of BPA leaching from the plastic into the water. Access to natural spring water that has been tested for purity is another excellent source. Fruit infused waters are another way to encourage you to drink your water. Keep a jug of water in your fridge infused with lemon slices or mint or other fruit, or cucumber—this will have you coming back for more!

Avoid or Reduce Consumption of Anti-nutrients

What are anti-nutrients? Anti-nutrients are those things that do not contribute to your overall health. They are not building blocks for your body. These include coffee, tea, caffeine, stimulants, carbonated beverages, sugar, artificial sweeteners, additives, preservatives, and alcohol. The pervasive use by the food manufacturing companies, especially with high fructose corn syrup, has caused many problems with our health. High fructose corn syrup is found in virtually all processed foods. These are empty calories without proper nutrition, and because the sugars take less time to digest, we feel hungry all the time. This programs us to consume more calories than we need. This leads to weight gain as our body stores the excess as fat. Over-consumption of sugar has resulted in many illnesses, nutritional deficiencies, mood swings, anxiety, depression and obesity in our society. Make the decision to cut down or eliminate refined sugars and processed foods, and replace them with real food. Become educated on how to read labels—as sugars have many different names—and recognize the names of additives and preservatives.

Eat Real, Wholesome, Unprocessed, Unrefined Foods

Bring health back into your life and the lives of your loved ones by creating healthy meals every day using fresh, whole foods. Our bodies deserve to function at their best, and we need to reclaim joy of eating real, wholesome food. Whole foods are foods that are as close to their natural state as possible. These include fresh colorful vegetables and fruits, nuts and seeds, whole grains, dried beans, wild salmon, free range grass fed beef, and wild meat. Whole foods have not undergone any processing, and therefore retain all of their nutrients and fibers. This balanced way of eating promotes lifelong health and vitality. Greens provide powerful phytochemicals and essential minerals that support the liver in its ability to increase production of antioxidants and excrete toxins from our body. Colorful vegetables also provide powerful antioxidants, vitamins, minerals, and essential fatty acids which we need on a daily basis.

An efficient functioning digestive system is key to our health. It is through digestion that our body receives the raw materials needed to nurture, repair, and fuel itself. Many unexplained and underlying symptoms such as bloating, heartburn, and flatulence, are the result of impaired digestion. Digestion starts in the mouth with the secretion of enzymes from our saliva, and it is therefore important that food is chewed thoroughly, and should not be diluted with too much fluid with the meal.

Healthy Fats

There are many misconceptions around the word *fat*. People have come to believe that fat is bad for you. There are bad fats which can cause health problems. These are the saturated and trans-fats which are common in processed foods and diets high in animal fats. These fats cause deficiencies of the essential fatty acids—the good fats. We require essential fatty acids for our cells, organs, and tissues. Essential fatty acids promote brain and eye development, and improve immune function and the optimal functioning of all our body systems.

What are the good fats and where are they found? These are found in nuts, seeds, wild fish, legumes, vegetables, and nut oils. Some examples are flaxseeds and flaxseed oil, wild salmon, sunflower seeds, almonds, hazelnuts, olive oil, and avocados. Organic coconut oil, although a saturated fat because it is solid at room temperature, is an excellent source of good fat. It is easily digestible and converted into quick energy rather than stored as fat in your body.

Healthy Start to the Day

The best way to start your day is to squeeze half a lemon into a glass of warm water and drink on an empty stomach, twenty minutes before you eat your breakfast. This helps to stimulate gastric juices, helps digestion, cleanses the liver, and boosts the immune system.

Eat a Healthy Breakfast

Breakfast can be as simple as a piece of fruit followed by a complex carbohydrate such as whole grains (oatmeal, for example). Nuts can be added for healthy fats. No time to prepare oatmeal? You can combine oatmeal with milk or almond milk in a jar the night before and put it in the fridge. In the morning top it with more milk or almond milk, nuts, seeds, or berries. You can take this with you to eat when you get to work. Avoid the simple carbohydrates such as prepared cereals, bagels, and muffins which all contain refined sugars.

Feed Your Spirit

Sit Up, Breath, And Embrace Life

Have more fun; practice meditation and relaxation techniques such as deep breathing exercises; develop good, meaningful relationships. These activities all help to reduce stress and bring more joy into your life. Find and experience self-love, self-respect, and self-worth. These are all part of Vitamin L— the love nutrient!

Be Joyful!

Practice gratitude in all that you do. Laugh! Laughter is a great stress release and is good for the body and soul. Laughter improves your mood and strengthens your immune system. Laughter also affects the people around you. Have you ever noticed when you hear someone laughing, you get that good mood feeling too?

Strive to maintain a good work-life balance. Ensure you take enough personal time to rejuvenate and focus on what is important to you.

Exercise

Exercise is very important to developing and maintaining a healthy body, as exercise promotes cell regeneration. Exercise, coupled with a healthy diet rich in nutrient dense whole foods, speeds up the rate of cell regeneration—an anti-aging strategy. Regular exercise also promotes sweat production, which helps cleanse the pores and promotes skin health. Make sure you have your water bottle with you to stay hydrated. Other benefits are: promoting body fat loss, muscle toning, cardiovascular health, and restful sleep.

You don't have to spend hours in the gym or run for hours, just maintain a consistent, daily routine of at least twenty minutes exercise such as walking, yoga, swimming, or playing with your children or grandchildren outdoors. Find something you enjoy doing and make it a routine. Put it in your schedule to keep you motivated, and keep your appointment with yourself. You are important. If you enjoy walking but want social contact, find a friend to walk with you and make an accountability agreement to keep you moving! Exercising outdoors has been associated with greater feelings of increased energy, revitalization, greater enjoyment, and satisfaction while decreasing stress and tension.

Peaceful Sleep

Good sleep allows your body to rest, recharge, and relieve stress. It is restoration time which will enable you to wake up feeling restored and energized for your day. It is important to create an environment that promotes good sleeping. Do an audit of your bedroom to identify anything that will disrupt your sleep. Studies have found that electromagnetic currents can contribute to the inability to rest or sleep deeply. Remove electric clock radios and cell phones from the head of the bed. Wi-Fi should not be in the bedroom or close to the bedroom. If it is close by, it should be shut off during the night.

Ensure your bedroom is dark, as sleeping in complete darkness allows your body to get into a deep phase of sleep. Take a warm bath in the evening and add Epsom salts and essential oils (for example, lavender) to it. This will help you relax before bedtime. Epsom salts are high in magnesium which is a tranquilizing mineral and added to your bath, helps your muscles relax. If you follow the above strategies, you should feel refreshed when you wake up, and ready to start your day.

It's That Simple!

If you follow the above strategies, you will feel energized and have the energy to live a healthy, joyful life.

Are you ready to start living an energized life? Take the next step and take advantage of the special offer below.

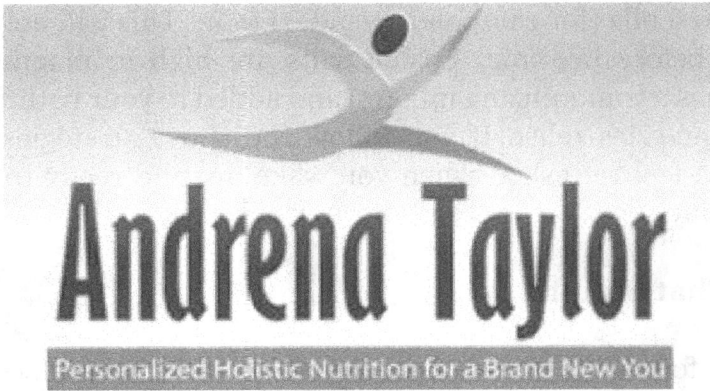

Andrena's Special Offer:

Receive Andrena's step-by-step guide,
5 Energy Boosters For A Brand New You
With simple strategies you can implement
right away for living an energized life at:

http://www.HolisticNutritionPlan.com

Bonus offer: once you register for
5 Energy Boosters For A Brand New You,
you receive a free *Fifteen-Minute Strategy Call*!

About Andrena Taylor

Andrena Taylor, RHN, is a Holistic Nutritionist, Healthy Lifestyle Coach, and a Meal and Menu Planning Expert from Canada. She is an educator whose goal is to empower and support people who are committed to realizing their health and wellness goals. She helps people on a path to increased energy, vitality and wellness.

She has a Bachelor of Arts degree in Sociology from the University of Calgary, Holistic Nutrition diploma from the Canadian School of Natural Nutrition, and is a member of eWomen Network. She is currently enrolled in the Professional Plant Based Certification course through Rouxbe, the world's leading online cooking school.

To find out more about Andrena, visit http://www.AndrenaTaylor.com

Chapter 10

Your WHY is Bigger Than You
by Shkira Singh

There I was, sitting at the corporate desk in a high rise building in downtown Los Angeles. I had always dreamed of moving up the corporate ladder and being a really successful business woman. But as I stared outside the window, looking at all the people walking in the courtyard, I couldn't help but wonder if they were happy with their jobs. I had achieved all my goals, and thought that when I got here, I would be truly happy. However, that was not the case at all; it was the total opposite because I felt empty coming into work. I had just received a "promotion" to work with high net worth clients, but I felt like the negative energy was sucking the life out of me. I'd walk into the office, happy and saying hello to everyone, with no one responding back to me. Everyone was stuck in their own cubicle, not wanting to look up— afraid you might want to talk to them. I felt like I was in the *Twilight Zone* and everyone were walking zombies.

I realized that I was meant to do more with my life and wanted to have more freedom. I decided that it would be to join my husband's practice. I was scared and worried because I failed at my last business, and I liked the security of working

117

for a big corporation. I had to let go of my fear and move forward. I wanted to have the benefits of a business owner, which include personal fulfillment, independence, and flexibility. And so began my journey.

I discovered a lot about myself and why I wanted to make the move to entrepreneurship. I asked myself many questions, and I learned some important things I believe all business owners should examine so they can be fully empowered as they move forward on their entrepreneurial path. I'd like to share five of those with you here.

1. What's Your Why?

Why are you in this business? Are you passionate about waking up every morning to go into your office? How are you making a true impact on your clients or employees? Having passion alone will not make a business profitable but it will be important when you are going through difficult times. Running a business is a form of artwork that you have to master every day.

When I opened my insurance agency, I quickly saw all that starting a business entailed. I opened the business thinking it would be great to do investments and cross-sell insurance to clients. I had never done property and casualty insurance before, but figured it would make a lot of profit. I wanted to have something that my children could one day help me run, or possibly sell the business if they weren't interested in running it. The problem was that I was not really passionate about being a financial advisor; and I did not really care about insurance. I just knew that I wanted to have freedom from the corporate politics and have a flexible schedule. I did not really care which business I opened as long as it would be profitable.

The happiest and most successful are the entrepreneurs are those who are in business for a reason larger than themselves. I believe this is because they are driven by passion and desire; something much deeper and more meaningful than just wanting to make a profit. I had never really discovered that when I entered the financial services world. My major in college was psychology, because I truly felt I could make a big impact on people's lives. However, I soon realized after doing many internships that I was drained every day, and felt as if I had the life sucked out of me. I could not imagine doing this for the rest of my life, and I did not know what else I could do.

I was working at a local bank during college and was moving up quickly because of my sales skills. I was soon offered a position as an assistant to a top financial advisor, and decided to take it since there was a potential to make a lot of money. I remember having conversations with the bosses multiple times, and I would leave those meetings feeling that I was not really making a big difference in the world. Everyone around me in the business thought I was crazy and that the money was so good it shouldn't matter. I chose to ignore the feelings I had deep down inside, and I continued my career for the next fifteen years. There came a point though, where it did not matter how much I made or how successful I was, I felt there was a void in my life.

You could have every material item you could possibly want, with all of your bills paid; and financial prosperity could be abundant in your life. But what is the *real reason—* the WHY—you are in business?

When you really understand your WHY, you can be tired, sick, have total chaos around you, and no matter what, your WHY and BELIEF are so strong, you will do whatever it takes to move your business forward. As we move forward in business and in life, we grow and change as individuals . . . our WHYs can be constantly changing! It's important to stay in touch with your WHY and go back to it often, as it will help you reach your successes and achievements.

Think about it: what is the reason (the WHY) you decided to start or join your business? What does that mean to you and what does that say about you as a person?

Here are two exercises that may help you reflect and discover your WHY:

1. ***Make a List.*** Create a list that you can keep it in your office by your desk. As you write, you'll see that a lot of the first things that come to mind in terms of your WHY are material things. You have to start at the surface, but then, scratch the surface deeper and deeper to go into the core of you. The deeper you go, ask, "*What else touches my heart?*" See which message in movies or books have touched your heart. What did you love doing in your childhood? Which tribe do you want to focus on and why? Meaning, who would be the ideal client you would like to work with, and why? You'll see that things will start to make, and you will get clear on what your why is. Keep your list with you, and when you find yourself in a moment of discouragement, or you don't want to do the things you need to, you will be quickly reminded of your WHY.

2. **Create a Vision Board.** When you create a vision board, you actually take ownership of your dreams, wants, wishes, and desires. Create a vision board for yourself that you can look at daily to remind you of WHY you do what you do each and every day. Simply

120

cut pictures out of magazines, newspapers, travel guides, etc.—anything that provides you with a visual of the dreams and desires you have. Look at your board every morning and every night. This will help you to move forward in your business. It's also important to do a vision board every year so you don't become comfortable, and so you are motivated to reach even higher goals than you did the previous year.

Knowing your WHY will help you zero in on the things that are most important to you in your business and personal life. Knowing what's important for you in your life will help you stay focused on the road ahead without letting obstacle's stop you in your business.

2. Study the Market/Business

Having a purpose and passion is important, but it will not guarantee a successful business. You need to study the business you want to enter and become an expert at knowing the ins and outs of it. Looking back, I realized that when I opened the insurance agency, I should have worked as an employee in one before I invested by life savings into it. I had no background of the business I was entering and I did not do my research. I decided that my district manger would be the best mentor and would guide me the right way. Little did I know that he was paid on recruiting new reps, not on my success. I made a lot of assumptions on things and did not spend the time to study the market or business. It's best that you work as an employee for at least a year in the business you would like to enter. I was not only learning on the job how to run a business, but also how the business worked. If I had worked for a company first, I would have been able to see if I liked the business *before* opening my location. I decided that I would open the store-front location in an area that was known for being competitive with the rates. I did not realize that the market had a lot of drawbacks. If I had talked with other agents in the area, I would have been able to be better prepared. I have learned that every time I sit down with another advisor in my field, I learn something to improve our systems and gain new ideas I would have never thought of.

Research Your Consumer

The best way to get that data is to get it yourself. Do your own research. Study the behavior of the clients you are focused on. For example, I did not take into account that the client market was known for not paying their insurance on time, and as a result policies would always have to be reissued, which was a lot of administrative work every month. Look at the goals you've set for yourself and analyze the products and/or services you offer. Think about how your products or services fulfill a need or solve a problem for a potential customer. Also, think about how you differ from other companies in your industry—what makes you stand out? Broadly think about who might be interested and who may benefit from having access to what you offer. Figuring out your selling point is the first step in identifying your ideal target audience.

Next, think about what information you need to know and why. What is it that you need to know about your potential customers in order to reach them?

As you consult your business plan and decide who you want your audience to be, remember that it is ultimately about the customer. Don't think about who you would like to sell to, think about who is looking for the products and services you offer.

After performing research, you'll want to create a customer profile. This is more than a brief statement; it's an in-depth description of who your typical customer may be and includes demographic and psychographic information:

- Demographic information: this may include age, gender, location, ethnic background, marital status, income, and more.

- Psychographic information: this type of information goes beyond the "external" and identifies more about a customer's psychology, interests, hobbies, values, attitudes, behaviors, lifestyle, and more.

Both types of information are essential for developing your customer profile. Demographic information will help you identify the type of person who will potentially buy your products and services. The work doesn't end after you've identified your target audience. It's essential to continually perform research to stay current on market and industry trends and your competition. It's also important to see if and how your current and potential customers evolve.

Before you begin marketing to your potential customers, make sure you know how you are going to track sales, interactions, requests for information, and more. Each one of these touch-points is important to record. This information will help you identify trends, patterns, and possible areas of improvement, which will continually help your marketing efforts as your business matures.

Understand Your Competition

Your next point of research will be your competition. Learn what they say and where they say it. You don't want to copy them, but you do want to be aware of what they're up to. If you can see firsthand their sales presentation, display, packaging, follow-up, and product itself, then you will be at a huge advantage, learning from top leaders what has been their major obstacles and best wins.

You need to know the ins and outs of your future endeavor. Try to find models that are proven to work, and get your ideas from there. Connect with business people who are in similar fields, and polish up on your business classes.

3. Budget

Having a budget is a key way to help you turn your dreams for business success into reality. This will help you track cash on hand, business expenses, and how much revenue you need to keep your business growing. By knowing and committing these numbers to paper, you increase your chances of succeeding with your business by anticipating future needs, spending, profits, and cash flow. It also may help you spot problems before it's too late, since you may not have enough money for emergencies. A budget for your business will help you figure out how much money you have, how much you need to spend, and how much you need to bring in to meet business goals. Budgets can also help you minimize risk to your business. A budget should first be created—before you invest in a business. Then, you can use this information to adjust your plans or expectations going forward. A twelve-month budget can be updated with actual expenditures and revenues each month so you know you're on target. If you're missing the targets set out in your budget, you can use the budget to figure out how you can reduce expenses, or you can increase sales by more aggressive marketing, or lower your profit expectations.

A budget should include:

Revenues, your costs, and your profits or surplus cash flow. A budget should be tabulated monthly. Sales and other revenue will help make these estimates as accurate as possible, but always be conservative if do not know the exact numbers. It is best to use your projected sales revenues or last year's actual sales figures. If you have a new business, you should research by asking other business people in the same field as you.

Total costs and expenses. Costs can be divided into categories: fixed, variable, and semi-variable:

- Fixed costs are those expenses that remain the same, whether or not your sales rise or fall.

- Variable costs correlate with sales volumes.

- Semi-variable costs are fixed costs that can be variable when influenced by volume of business.

Profits: the dollar amount of revenue minus total costs equals profit. Once you have profit estimates, you can start to see if you can afford to expand or invest in other areas of the business.

4. Forecast

Your sales forecast is the backbone of your business plan. People measure a business and its growth by sales, and your sales forecast sets the standard for expenses, profits and growth. The sales forecast is almost always going to be the first set of numbers you'll track for *plan vs. actual use.* This is what you'll do even if you do no other numbers.

Forecasting is mainly educated guessing. So don't expect to get it perfect; just make it reasonable. There's no business owner who isn't qualified to forecast sales if you have done your research. Business owners work hard every day to grow their business and make it a success. It is important not to get caught up in the day-to-day operations and neglect to take into account long-term strategy and planning.

You can start by forecasting unit sales per month. Not all businesses sell by units, but see how you can break things down in your business to get a sales number. For example, accountants and attorneys sell hours, taxis sell rides, and restaurants sell meals.

Whenever you have past sales data, your best forecasting aid is the most recent data. Get started by projecting your two most recent years of sales, by month.

Forecasting income is important if you want your business model to run smoothly. In doing so, companies can quickly see if they have efficient overhead, are pricing their products and services correctly, and what their gross profit margin is.

5. Monitor Activity Level

Tracking and publishing your numbers tells employees what's important. For example, if you track customer satisfaction, number of refunds, and average customer hold times, your customer service manager knows precisely how he is being judged and what to improve.

Keep in mind: don't just look at your numbers to determine what needs fixing. Use them to pinpoint what's working well in your business and do more of that.

Most entrepreneurs don't know these details. Yet if you start to track and understand the numbers in your business, you can quickly increase your sales and profits. Research indicates organizations which set goals are much more likely to achieve them. However, to achieve a goal, you must be able to properly measure your progress. By understanding how your business is doing in both revenues and profits daily, you can tell if you're on track to achieve your goals, and you can adjust your plans as needed if you're not. There are a handful of smaller activities that effect larger results. For example, the following are often key underlying issues for sales:

- Number of outbound sales calls

- Number of live connections

- Number of proposals given

- Proposal close rate

- Average price per sale

When sales are low, most entrepreneurs don't know what to fix to see improvement. By tracking each of these numbers, you can instantly know what to fix. Most entrepreneurs have a bad sales month, then look back to determine what caused it. Had the entrepreneur tracked his numbers on the underlying issues, he could have fixed the problem early on. For example, he might have learned that the number of proposals issued in the first week of the month was low, and made sure more proposals went out the door. By understanding and tracking your numbers, you can measure whether your business is performing well.

Monitoring activity is KEY to the success of your organization. Was the number of sales contacts per week important to the success of your organization?

It is related to PERFORMANCE when it can be clearly measured, quantified, and easily influenced by the members of your team. It is used as an INDICATOR; in other words, it is something that provides leading information about future results. It might be a good idea to track the number of calls and the amount of time each sales maker spends with high value contacts in those accounts, and set some specific expectations there that can be measured.

Key Performance Indicators (KPI's) should provide visibility into current activity that will impact future sales-team productivity. Tracking these indicators in the present will allow you to identify gaps and coach your team members, which will help you influence the outcome of those monthly, quarterly, and annual productivity numbers that are so important. *Key Performance Indicators* are quantifiable measurements, agreed to beforehand, that reflect the critical success factors of an organization. They will differ depending on the organization.

Tracking KPIs is the best way to identify and qualify sales maker performance. Sales people might be staying busy and giving a one hundred percent effort every day, which can be mistaken for real productivity. Tracking KPIs helps organizations make sure sales makers are spending the right amount of time on the right activities.

The best businesses are not those that focus on merely earning money, but those that are clear about what their main purpose is. It is important for business owners to plan and budget in advance in order for the business to remain stable and grow. It is also important to have data for your business to understand that market and consumer. Taking these five steps will help you avoid the errors that lead to most businesses failing.

About Shkira Singh

Shkira Singh is a Financial Advisor at LPL Financial in the Los Angeles area. She has been a trusted advisor to her clients, both individuals and businesses, for over fourteen years. She focuses on advising high net worth individuals with retirement income planning and wealth preservation, as well as estate and family asset transfer strategies.

Shkira lives in Northridge, California with her husband and two children. She enjoys spending time with her family and has a true passion for travel, hoping to explore as many countries and cultures as she can in her lifetime.

A Final Note from
Tracy Repchuk

Thank you for your investment in this book, and for the continuing relationship you will have with me and the co-authors. We are dedicated to serving you and your needs and look forward to our journey together with you.

You can ***claim all of your free gifts from this book*** at **www.EmpowerBusinessEverywhere.com** where all the author's gifts can be found in one place.

Enjoy the journey and stay in touch.

To Your Ongoing Success,

Tracy Repchuk
5-Time International Bestselling Author and Speaker

*If you would like to become a published author
and be in a book like this with me, go to
www.QuantumLeapAuthor.com
and take your next step.*